# Sea-Road of the Saints

# Celtic Holy Men in the Hebrides

John Marsden

# Sea-Road of the Saints

## Celtic Holy Men in the Hebrides

Floris Books

First published in 1995 by Floris Books

The author gratefully acknowledges the generosity
of Caledonian MacBrayne Ltd in sponsoring his
research along the Sea-Road of the Saints.

The publisher acknowledges subsidy from the Scottish
Arts Council towards the publication of this volume.

British Library CIP Data available

ISBN 0-86315-210-4

Printed in Great Britain
by Biddles Ltd, Guildford

For my wife Jenni

# Contents

Maps 8

Preface 11

Introduction 13
The White Martyrdom and the Western Sea
*The coming of Christianity 15; Celtic Ireland 24; The ancient Irish Church 27; The legacy of Irish tradition 32; Celtic Scotland 39; Sea-road of the Saints 44*

Kintyre 47
"A Grey Eye upon Erin"
*Columba's "pilgrimage to Britain" 48; The kingdom of Dalriada 54; The historical St Columba 58; The pilgrimage of Ciaran of Saigir 63*

Islay 71
"Blue-green Ile"
*The miracle of St Cainnech's crozier 72; Kilarrow and Maelrubha 79; Kilmeny and Eithne 83; Kilchoman and Comman 86; The enigma of Kildalton 91; "The Island of St Finlaggan" 97*

Jura                                          99
"The Island of Hinba"
  *The quest for "Hinba" 101; The burial-place of*
  *Ernan 104; Columba's visions on Hinba 107; The*
  *Eucharist of the Abbots 114*


Iona                                         129
"I-Columcille"
  *The holy island of the western sea 130; Iona in*
  *Dalriada 134; The evidence of Adamnan 137; Iona*
  *on the sea-road 141*


The Outer Hebrides and Beyond                145
"In search of a Hermitage in the Ocean"
  *Hermits of the Ocean 150; Beccan of Rhum 152;*
  *Cormac of the Sea 153; Moluag of Lismore 162;*
  *Brendan the Voyager 165; The sea-road to "farthest*
  *Thule" 184*


Afterword                                    189
The Descent of the Red Martyrdom


References                                   197
A Hebridean Calendar of Saints               199
Chronology                                   201
Bibliography                                 205
Index                                        211

*Beloved are Durrow and Derry,*
*Beloved is pure Raphoe,*
*Beloved is Drumhome the fruitful,*
*Beloved are Swords and Kells;*
*But sweeter and lovelier far*
*The salt sea where the sea-gulls fly.*

TRADITIONALLY ATTRIBUTED TO ST COLUMBA.

*(Durrow, Derry, Raphoe, Drumhome, Swords and Kells were the principal Columban monasteries in Ireland.)*

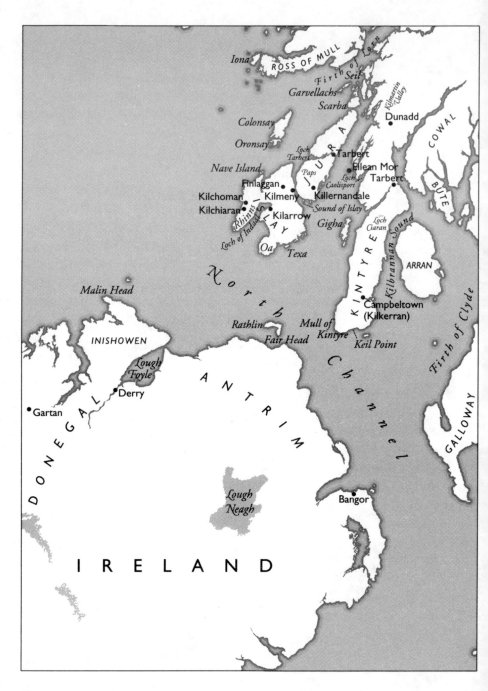

*Map of the Inner Hebrides*

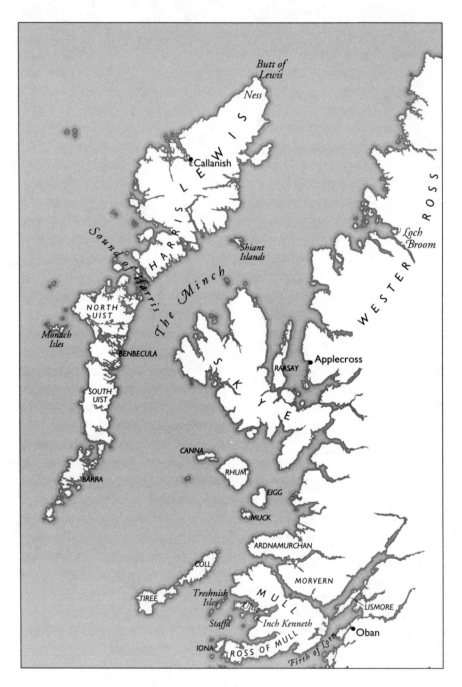

Map of the Outer Hebrides

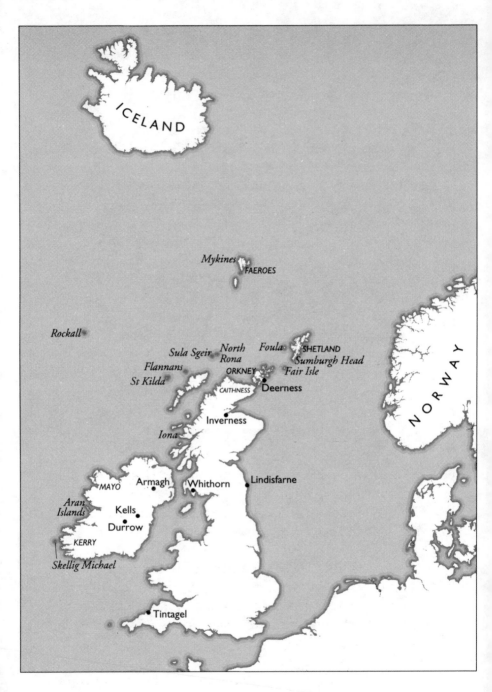

*Map of the Sea-Road of Saints*

# PREFACE

I call to mind now the sea-crossing from Kennacraig on
Kintyre to Port Askaig on the island of Islay through a
grey September afternoon some two years past. On
every hand were ranged the most ancient landscapes of
Celtic Scotland while away to the south and almost
visible on the farthest horizon lay the Heads of Antrim
and the land of Ireland.

The holy man Columcille is said to have spoken of "a
grey eye that will look back upon Erin" when he sailed
these same waters more than fourteen hundred years
ago on voyage to his destiny as St Columba of Iona.
The monochrome seascape of that afternoon seemed to
mirror his words with the most striking precision and
led me to think of the very many holy men out of
Ireland who passed this way, in Columcille's wake and
before him, through the distant centuries when the
islands of the Hebrides marked out a sea-road of the
saints. It was, as I recall, that thought on that afternoon which has led me to this book.

From the Mull of Kintyre to the Butt of Lewis, place-
name dedications commemorating saints almost beyond
counting, ruined medieval chapels built on the sites of
still more ancient hermitages and stone-carved crosses
more than a thousand years old, chart the progress of
Irish holy men along the full extent of the western
seaboard of what is now Scotland. If the evidence of
these holy places of the western sea were to be brought

together with the evidence of the annals, martyrologies and *Lives* of saints which comprise the wealth of early sources for the history of the ancient Irish church, it might be possible to construct some genuinely historical account of the three-hundred-year pilgrimage of Celtic holy men along the sea-road which led from Ireland to Iona and beyond.

Such was, indeed still is, the first intention of *Sea-Road of the Saints* and while I knew at the time of framing such an intention that a book drawing on a decade of personal pilgrimages would be written from an inevitably personal perspective, I was not to know then that I would have made my home in the Western Isles by the time I came to write it. If that accident of a writer's life has played any part of its own in what follows here, I can only hope that it might have helped illuminate this account of Celtic holy men in the Hebrides with something of that same light on land and sea which so richly infuses all that we know of their voyages and visions.

JM

# INTRODUCTION
# The White Martyrdom and the Western Sea

*This is the white martyrdom to man,*
*when he separates from everything he loves,*
*though he suffer fasting and labour thereat.*
THE CAMBRAI HOMILY

Sometime in the second half of the eighth century, a continental scribe working to a commission from the bishop of Cambrai made a copy of a book of Irish canons — or monastic laws — written in Latin and very possibly originating on Iona.

None of which would have been at all remarkable, Irish learning having been renowned and Irish books highly prized in European monasteries for some two hundred years, had it not been for an apparent accident of scribal inattention on this occasion. At some point in this book's travels, a page from another and much older manuscript containing a homily written in the Old Irish of the late seventh century had been left, perhaps as a bookmark, inserted between its leaves. Whether or not he noticed the disruption of sense or even the change of language, our scribe diligently copied out each page as he came to it — passing from

Latin to Old Irish and back again to Latin — and in so
doing rescued for posterity the oldest surviving example of continuous Irish prose.

It is this text, now known as the "Cambrai Homily,"
which preserves the earliest record of the three orders
of martyrdom — the white martyrdom of exile, the
green martyrdom of the hermit and the red martyrdom
of blood sacrifice — held by the Irish church to be
"precious in God's eyes, for which we obtain rewards if
we fulfil them." It would, in fact, have been more than
fitting if the original manuscript fragment transcribed
as the *Cambrai Homily* had been set down on Iona,
because the three ideals of martyrdom which it describes would seem now, each of them in its turn and
time, to mark out the great themes of the history of the
Celtic holy man in the western sea.

With the exception of one isolated instance, the red
martyrdom is almost entirely absent from the annals of
Ireland until the ferocious onslaught of the viking raids
in the last years of the eighth century. Examples of the
green martyrdom, by contrast, are to be found throughout the lives and traditions of the Irish saints and
especially in the islands of the Hebrides, where the
quest of the holy man for a "desert place in the ocean"
echoed the earliest origins of monasticism in the deserts of third-century Egypt. Yet it is the white martyrdom which takes precedence in the *Cambrai Homily*
and with good reason, because it was the white martyrdom of exile from homeland and kindred which is presented by all the earliest sources as the spiritual
imperative for the great pilgrimage of the Celtic saints
into the western sea.

The ideal of the white martyrdom formalized the
tenet of *peregrinatio* or "pilgrimage for Christ," by
which the holy man sought to separate himself from

every worldly tie in order that he might pursue the single-minded quest for God on earth. It was a tradition singularly characteristic of the ancient Irish church and as old as the very earliest evidences for Christianity in Ireland, but the deepest roots of its significance must be sought, as must those of the sea-road itself, in the still more ancient context of Celtic Ireland.

# The coming of Christianity

The term "Celtic Church" is dismissed by scholars as historically meaningless — and for the best of historical reasons — because at no point in history was there any such institution. Indeed, the early churches of the Celtic peoples in the west differed in at least as many ways as they resembled each other, yet "Celtic Church" continues in popular usage where it serves, in almost every instance, as a synonym for the more historically meaningful term "ancient Irish church." While that popular usage falls short of precise historical accuracy, it does, nonetheless, acknowledge the wide scholarly recognition of the ancient Irish church as representing the unique encounter of an essentially intact Celtic druidic culture with the man-god whom the Celt recognized in Christ.

The initial circumstances of that encounter remain so impenetrable an enigma that even the eminent historian of Celtic Ireland, Ludwig Bieler, has admitted that "we do not know when or in what way the Irish first came into contact with Christianity."[1] What can be said with absolute certainty, by reason of Ireland having been separated from mainland Britain a thousand years before Britain was separated from continental

Europe, is that the contact can only have come about by sea.

The most extraordinary, yet still far from implausible, possibility is that the new faith came to Ireland by a direct route from its eastern wellsprings. The eighth-century Irish *Litany of Pilgrim Saints* includes an invocation of the "Seven monks of Egypt in Diseart Uilaig" — a site tentatively identified as Dundesert near Crumlin in Antrim — and raises the remarkable prospect of Egyptian monks finding their way to Ireland along seaways which had even then been known to Mediterranean navigators for three thousand years. Glass fragments of Egyptian origin and with no Roman connection have been excavated at Tintagel in Cornwall. They have been dated to the third century AD — which would make them almost precisely contemporary with the emergence of monasticism in Egypt — and must have been brought to Cornwall along the same sea-road which had been in regular use by Phoenician tin traders plying the Cornish coast as early as the sixth century BC.

If Egyptian glassware could reach Cornwall in the third century after Christ, there is no reason why holy men out of the Egyptian desert should not have continued further along the same prehistoric seaway to make landfall in Ireland. If, indeed, they had done so, it would well explain why so many Irish hermits in search of retreat from the world should have been seeking a "desert place" in the ocean, how variant gospel readings known to derive from the Desert Fathers came into Irish usage, how Coptic textual forms found their way into the seventh-century *Book of Dimma* from Tipperary, and why the third-century St Antony of Egypt features so prominently in the carvings on the high crosses at Kells and Monasterboice.

Whatever the plausibility of the Egyptian connection, the greater probability must be that the initial contact of the Irish with Christianity was made by way of their Celtic cousins in Gaul. Indeed, the enigmatic eastern components in the early Irish church might just as probably have derived from Gaul where the new faith out of the Mediterranean had established its first firm foothold in western Europe before the last quarter of the second century AD. The concentration of the earliest evidence for Irish Christianity in the south and east of the island and the especial veneration in Ireland of St Martin, the fourth-century bishop of Tours and the pioneer of monasticism in the west, both point impressively to a Gaulish inspiration flowing along the ancient sea-road which had served trading links, and with them cultural exchanges, between western Gaul and the Irish Sea since the pre-Roman Iron Age.

From Gaul, Christianity had penetrated throughout Rome's western empire — evidently more greatly aided by the imperial network of routes and roads than it was impeded by oppression from pagan emperors — and the evidence of St Alban, who suffered the first recorded martyrdom of Roman Britain sometime around AD 209, confirms a Christian presence to have been established in *provincia Britannica* at least as early as the first years of the third century.

Ireland, of course and unlike Britain and Gaul, lay beyond the western boundary of Roman conquest. Despite the ambition of Agricola who had looked across the North Channel from the coast of Galloway in the last quarter of the first century AD and contemplated the possibility of invasion, the Roman war-machine which had conquered the greater expanse of Europe west of the Rhine shrank back from the crossing of the Irish Sea. Unconquered by the Roman imperium and

very largely untouched by Roman influence, Celtic
Ireland seems nonetheless to have been rarely out of
touch with Roman Britain. Irish raiders, called *Scotti*
by the Latin historians, had begun to harass the
mainland by the mid-third century and, quite certainly,
included Christians amongst the slaves they brought
back to Ireland, but contacts between Celtic Ireland
and Roman Britain had been recorded since the later
first century — when Agricola is known to have met
with an Irish chieftain driven into exile on the mainland — and were by no means all hostile. There is a
mounting body of archaeological evidence for trading as
well as raiding across the Irish Sea and evidence also
for Irish warriors employed as mercenaries in Roman
service, all of which would have brought the Irish into
various degrees of contact with Romano-British Christians, as indeed would the Irish attempts to colonize
parts of Wales and Cornwall on the western fringes of
Roman Britain in the later fourth century.

Such then were the possible channels along which
the Christian faith entered into Celtic Ireland, each of
them perhaps playing its own part at some stage in the
process and all of them following sea-roads known for
millennia to the prehistoric cultures out of which had
emerged the maritime peoples of the west.

The one possibility which has not so far been considered here is the popular tradition which credits "St
Patrick" with the single-handed conversion of the Irish
to Christianity in the first half of the fifth century and
which is flatly denied by all the evidence. It is, nonetheless, true that if history is to be defined as the
reconstruction of the past from its documentary record
then the history of Ireland begins with the historical
Patrick, who called himself by the Latin name-form of

*Patricius* and who was the author of the two most ancient documents known to have been written in Ireland. In the first of these, known as his *Letter to Coroticus,* Patricius declares himself to be "a bishop" resident in Ireland and threatens the warlord Coroticus — most plausibly identified as Ceretic, the first historical king of the Britonic kingdom of Strathclyde — with excommunication for apostasy, upbraiding him for the seizure of newly-converted Irish Christians from the bishop's own flock in the course of a slave-taking raid on Ireland. The more substantial *Confessio,* set down by Patricius in his old age, is a primarily spiritual testament shot through with biblical references and supernatural visions and devoid of dates or any proper names which can be corroborated with other sources, but it does contain those fragments of autobiography which preserve almost all of what is known about the historical Patrick.

He was a Romano-Briton from Bannavem Taburniae — a place-name which appears on no known map of Roman Britain but which is most plausibly located on the north-west coast between the Clyde and the Solway — who had been carried off into slavery at the age of sixteen by the Irish raiders who preyed on a Britain abandoned by the legions in AD 410. His family were evidently Christian because his grandfather had been a priest, but Patricius himself, on his own confession, "did not know the true God" until his time of slavery as a herd-boy in Ireland. He offers no explanatory detail of his conversion, but portrays himself as a devout Christian when he made his escape, found his way to the coast and there took ship from Ireland. "After a few years" — which may have been spent in Gaul although Patricius does not say so — he was back in Britain and there experienced the vision in which the people of

Ireland appealed to him to return to live amongst them. So it was that Patricius, "a sinner, most unlearned, the least of all the faithful, and utterly despised by many," came to spend the rest of his days in Ireland and to pass from history into tradition as its national apostle.

These two documents, both of them authenticated as the work of the same man in the later fifth century AD, comprise the sum of contemporary evidence for the historical Patrick. It was to be another two hundred years before the saint reappeared in the early sources, as the subject of the two *Lives* by Muirchú and Tírechán, by which time he had become established as the founding saint of the church of Armagh and, still more significantly, as the "Apostle of Ireland." Another two centuries divide those seventh-century Lives from the Old Irish *Tripartite Life* in which the Romano-Briton bishop Patricius appears to have been recast, if not entirely re-invented, in the mould of the ancient Irish church as Pátraic, "the head of the belief of the Gael."[2]

The Patrick legend, driven by the political, ecclesiastical and theological imperatives of early medieval Ireland, may well preserve genuine historical traditions amongst a welter of later contrivances but this is not the place in which to attempt to extricate the one from the other. It must be said, however, that if the historical Patricius was the first casualty of the burgeoning cult of "St Patrick, Apostle of Ireland," he was certainly not the only one. There is evidence in the calendars of saints and medieval *Lives* deriving from earlier sources to indicate a number of holy men, recognized by historians as the "pre-Patrician" saints — not least among them Ciaran of Saigir and Ailbe of Emly, both of whom will be of further interest here — who were certainly contemporaries, even elder contemporaries, of the historical Patrick. Their territories lay in the southern half of Ireland and their enduring traditions very evidently posed a problem for the promoters of the Patrick legend who seem to have gone to great lengths to present these elder saints of Ireland as native bishops ordained by "St Patrick" as his delegate missionaries in the south. The greater historical probability is that these elder saints of Ireland were quite independent of Patrick's activities in the north and were, in fact, the heirs to a Christianity which had reached Ireland along the sea-road from Gaul at least as early as the fourth century AD.

The Irish annals, all of them medieval or later compilations from more ancient sources, are in full agreement that the date of Patrick's foundation of Armagh — and by implication his return to Ireland — was AD 432. It is at least unlikely that the annalists had any reliable authority for such a date, which has been convincingly proposed as a fusion of Celtic mystical numerology with the cycles of the classical calendars, and the great weight of modern historical opinion would place Patrick's years in Ireland in the second half of the fifth century. Even if the traditional date of 432 for Patrick's arrival in Ireland were to be accepted, there is still nowhere any historical doubt that Christianity had reached Ireland long before Patrick came — if, in fact, he did come — to Armagh.

The reliable fifth-century Gaulish chronicle of Prosper of Aquitaine enters the year 431 as the date when Pope Celestine ordained one Palladius — of whom virtually nothing else is known — to be sent "to the Irish believing in Christ as their first bishop." The purpose of Palladius' mission to Ireland, like those of the Gaulish bishops Germanus of Auxerre and Lupus of Troyes to mainland Britain at much the same time,

was to counter the heresy which had emerged out of
the Celtic west to throw the early fifth-century church
into theological turmoil. This "Pelagian" heresy — an
assertion of the spiritual power of human free will
independent of divine grace which has been best
summarized in modern times as "an individual path to
the Christ mystery"[3] — is named for its principal
advocate, the extraordinary holy man known as Pelagius who outraged Augustinian orthodoxy when he
arrived in Rome around the year AD 394.

The central significance of Pelagius here is that not
only was he a Celt, but apparently — on the evidence
of his most outspoken theological antagonist, St Jerome, who derided him as "heavy with Irish porridge" —
an Irish Celt. Whether or not Pelagius actually came
from Ireland, and most recent scholarship suggests he
was from the Irish settlement in south Wales, is less
important here than the fact that Jerome was able to
believe that he did and, by implication, to recognize
Christianity as sufficiently long-established in Ireland
by the last decade of the fourth century to produce so
dramatic and disruptive a heresiarch at least a generation before Patrick.

Neither was Patricius the first holy man to find his
way to Ireland from North Britain, because there is a
curious fragment of evidence that he was preceded by
the shadowy but significant figure of St Ninian. An
immediate contemporary of Pelagius, Ninian founded
his monastery at Whithorn on the Solway around the
year 397. Some number of Irish saints are said to have
studied there and it was a foundation known to have
been held in high esteem by the Irish church of the
sixth century and later, but the contact between
Whithorn and Ireland may well have been initiated in
its founder's own lifetime. While Ninian's obituary is

nowhere recorded by the early sources, the date of his death is traditionally placed at 423 and an Old Irish *Life* of Ninian tells how he left Britain some time after founding Whithorn to spend his last years in Ireland, where his feast-day is commemorated on the 16th of September in the eighth-century calendar of saints compiled by Oengus the Culdee.

Whenever and however the first contact had been made, Christianity had already established a presence in Ireland before the end of the fourth century, even though little, if anything, is known of the form that it took.

The writings of the historical Patrick are the principal contemporary source for what is known of the church in fifth-century Ireland and they indicate a primitive replica of the Roman ecclesiastical organization, where a lay community of believers worship under the pastoral care of a bishop. Although the Irish annals cannot agree on the date of Patrick's death, those set down in the eleventh century by Tigernach, abbot of Clonmacnois, concur most closely with modern scholarly opinion in placing Patrick's obituary at 493. At which point in history, the sources for Irish Christianity fall almost entirely silent for at least a generation. The rapidly advancing settlement of what had been Rome's *provincia Britannica* by the pagan Angles, Saxons and other Germanic peoples cut Ireland off from mainland Britain through most of the sixth century, much as the collapse of Rome's western empire and the infestation of the seaways by Germanic pirates had greatly impaired, if not completely severed, communications between Ireland and Gaul a hundred years earlier.

Ireland had thus become more isolated from the

outside world than ever before and when Irish Christianity re-enters the full light of history in the middle
decades of the sixth century, it has taken on the
characteristically "Celtic" form of the ancient Irish
church.

While very many of the qualities which have been
claimed in modern times for the "Celtic Church" are
clearly derived from genuine characteristics of the
ancient Irish church, they are very often highly coloured, if not greatly distorted, by the perspective of
hindsight. Just as there was no such institution as the
"Celtic Church," neither was there any such theological
phenomenon as "Celtic Christianity" because there is
nowhere any evidence that any Celtic church believed
itself to have been anything other than a completely
orthodox part of the wider Christian church with which
it shared with every fundamental of the same faith
founded on the same gospels. Those points on which
the practices of the early Irish church differed from the
Roman orthodoxy came about by reason of Ireland's
isolation from the continent through the turbulence of
the Dark Ages and resulted in the Irish retaining
earlier Christian practices which had at one time also
prevailed in the continental church. What is so often
seen now as the especial "Celtic" complexion of the
ancient Irish church derives not from its theology but
from its social and cultural context of Celtic Ireland.

# Celtic Ireland

These people we call Celts first enter history as the
*Keltoi* in the writings of classical historians. Whether
or not it was the name they called themselves, as

Caesar certainly believed it to be, its original meaning has never been firmly identified. It may well, like *Galli* or "Gauls," have derived from a vernacular term for "warrior," because the Celts did emerge out of the great prehistoric invasion by Indo-European warrior tribes who had swept out of Asia Minor and across Europe to reach the western edge of its Atlantic seaboard in the course of the first millennium BC. For all the many and various later usages of the term "Celtic," it can only be used as a cultural identity, because the Celts are most strictly defined as peoples sharing two forms of the same prehistoric Celtic mother tongue, the "insular Celtic" Goidelic, which has since become Scots and Irish Gaelic, and the "continental Celtic" Britonic, from which Welsh, Cornish and Breton are descended.

Prehistorians are greatly at variance as to when and how the first Celtic people reached Ireland. Estimates range from as early as 1600 BC in the later Bronze Age to the middle centuries of the first millennium BC, by which time the Goidelic Celts — who are believed to have comprised the first wave of fully-formed Celtic settlement to reach these islands — had established themselves, with their sophisticated agriculture and revolutionary metalworking, as the dominant culture of the Irish Iron Age.

Celtic Ireland, then, emerges out of prehistory in very much the same form as it was to survive until the impact of the vikings in the ninth century AD. It was a society principally sustained by an agricultural economy and where wealth was reckoned in cattle. A society without coinage, without towns or cities, and with no roads such as those built in Roman Britain for the march of the imperial legions, Ireland would have appeared barbaric, even primitive, to a fifth-century Roman Briton such as Patricius who did, in fact,

describe himself to Coroticus as "living among bar-
barians."

For all that and while the towns and villas of former
Roman Britain crumbled under the onslaught of the
Germanic warbands advancing along the roads built for
the legions, Celtic Ireland represented a sophisticated
and long-established civilization in a Europe engulfed
by the Dark Ages. It was a hierarchical society structured, as it had been for the greater part of a millennium, on blood-kinship. The primary social unit was
the extended family, or *fine,* some number of which
were brought together into the primary political unit of
the tribal clan, or *túath.* At the head of each *túath*
stood its king or *rí,* whose stature derived from his
membership of the ruling *fine.* Below the *rí* were
ranked his own noble kindred and beside them the
learned class which included the *brehons* or lawmakers,
the bards guarding the time-honoured traditions and
genealogies of the tribe, and the druids who formed the
priesthood of pre-Christian Ireland. The hierarchy
descended then through the craftsmen, most prominent
amongst them those endowed with their own magical
aspect who worked in metal, to the lower orders of
humbler landowners and labourers, and finally to the
slaves.

By the later fifth century of Patrick's time in Ireland,
the greater dynasties had emerged and the *rí* of the
*túath* acknowledged the *ruirí,* or "great king," as his
overlord within a tribal confederacy. He, in turn, owed
formal allegiance — at least on such occasions as he
chose to pay it — to the *ard rí,* or "high king," whose
power reflected the supremacy achieved by his dynasty
over its rivals in battle. The warlike character of such
a society, and also its enthusiasm for cattle-raiding,
was reflected by the strongholds of the tribal kings —

in the form of the hillfort, or *dún,* and the ring-fort, or *rath,* defended by an encircling bank and ditch — which represented the symbols of the power of the *túath* across the landscape of ancient Ireland.

# The ancient Irish Church

In distinct contrast to the episcopal structure of the Romano-British church, which took its shape from the urban organization of Roman imperial society, the ancient Irish church which had emerged by the mid-sixth century represented, initially by virtue of its essentially monastic character, the mirror image of Celtic Ireland.

Monasticism had emerged in the second half of the third century when holy men fled into the Egyptian desert, first to escape Roman persecution but afterwards as a reaction against the decadence of the later Empire, there to pursue the life of the ascetic hermit. Paul of Thebes is traditionally believed to have been the first hermit, but his stature has been overshadowed by his better-known friend and contemporary, Antony of Egypt, who spent twenty years living entirely alone in an abandoned desert fortress before relinquishing his solitude to gather together a number of like-minded disciples and form them into the first monastic community. Many more holy men were inspired to follow his example, initially in the eastern deserts but very soon afterwards in the western Empire, where Martin of Tours founded his first monastery in Gaul little more than a decade after Antony's death. At the time of Martin's death in 397, Ninian was building his monastic church at Whithorn on the Solway and it would seem that the monastic ideal must have also reached

Ireland, if not directly from its Egyptian wellsprings
then from Gaul, at very much the same time.

The monasteries of the ancient Irish church were
closely similar in almost every way to those of the
Desert Fathers, and yet, of course, dramatically different from those of later medieval centuries. The monk
— a term deriving from the Greek *monachos* which
translates as "living alone" — was not necessarily a
priest, but he was, by definition, one who had chosen
the solitary life and the earliest monasteries, whilst
formed for reasons of mutual security or survival, were
first established as communities of solitaries. Each
member would have his own simple circular dwelling
or cell — much akin to the humbler forms of secular
housing — where he would observe the liturgical offices
of the day in the assured knowledge that his brother
monks were performing precisely the same psalms and
prayers at just the same time. The simplest monasteries, thus, had no essential need for any form of church
and where there was such a building — customarily
built, as were the monastic cells, of wood and wattle —
the community may well have chosen only to gather
there together for worship on Sundays or days of
festival significance. Even when monasteries developed,
as they had certainly done in Ireland by the mid-sixth
century, into largely self-sustaining communities —
wherein the discipline of labour supplanted self-deny-
ing solitude and "to work was to pray" — the monk
who chose to separate himself from the community was
revered for his pursuit of the "green martyrdom."

Monasticism, then, formed the core of the ancient
Irish church and, in so doing, reflected the structure of
secular Irish society in a way that an episcopal church
could never have done, because the monastic community, or *familia,* represented the counterpart of the

*túath.* So too, the monastic *vallum,* or the boundary
bank and ditch which enclosed the cells of the monks,
cast the early Irish monastery into the form of a *rath*
and, indeed, many early monasteries were sited within
the defences of former ring-forts. The relationship
between the monastic *familia* and the secular *túath*
went beyond such mere semblance, because the blood-
kinship which bonded the social unit of Celtic Ireland
fulfilled the same role within the *familia.* The saints of
Ireland were, all of them, creatures of a tribal society
and many, although by no means all, were of noble
lineage. Members of the monastic community were
drawn from the same *túath,* if not the *fine* and in many
cases from the *derbfine,* or immediate blood-kin, as the
founding saint, and the land for the monastery was
granted to its founder by his tribal king and was
recognized as the personal property of the saint. Thus,
the abbots who succeeded him, customarily chosen from
descendants of his own *fine,* were known as his *comar-
bai,* literally "co-heirs" to his foundation. The authority
of the abbot, as the *comarba* of the founding saint, was
supreme — taking precedence over that of a bishop in
such areas of early Christian Ireland where there was
an episcopal office — and represented the ecclesiastical
counterpart of the power of the tribal king. Much as
the *familia* reflected the *túath,* and the abbot the *rí,* so
the monastic confederation, or *paruchia,* which brought
together each saint's lesser foundations under the aegis
of his principal church, corresponded to the secular
dynasty, and not least when *paruchiae* became entangled in their own rivalries and conflicts.

Against such a background, and for all the monastic
ideal of withdrawal from the world, it was inevitable
that the ancient Irish church should have become

involved in the customarily turbulent political life of
early medieval Ireland. Even as soon as their first
entry into the light of history in the sixth century, the
saints of Ireland are portrayed by the early sources as
men possessed of political as well as spiritual power,
appearing by turns as advisor and antagonist of kings
and high-kings, even on one occasion as king-maker,
and in so doing, the Christian holy man had already
taken up the role which had formerly been the domain
of the druid.

The origin of the name "druid" is obscure, but it has
been plausibly suggested as deriving from *drui,* or
"man of knowledge," and the man of knowledge has,
since distant antiquity, been also the man of power. In
the *mórdáil,* the great council of Celtic Ireland, the
druid spoke first and the king after him, because the
druid spoke with the voice of the otherworld of departed ancestors and ancients. He was the shaman of
the Celts of the west, the seer who knew all that was,
all that had been and all that was yet to come.

His power hinged on secrecy, because druidic learning was never committed to writing, but passed instead, by word of mouth and power of memory, to each
succeeding generation of a learned élite and was
effectively doomed when the coming of Christianity
brought with it a tradition of learning founded on the
written word. Nonetheless, the formerly druidic order
of bards survived to take its own prominent place in
early Christian Ireland and the druids themselves
survived the arrival of Christianity by at least two
centuries before they were entirely superseded by the
Christian holy man. Throughout those two centuries,
druid and saint would seem to have co-existed, if not in
harmony then at least without bloodletting, because
there is nowhere any evidence of persecution of Chris-

tians in early Ireland. Whenever a clash between saint
and druid is recorded in the early sources it centres on
political rivalry and on those occasions in the *Lives* of
the saints when the holy man engages in a wonder-
working contest with a druid rival, he emerges as the
Christian victor always by out-matching pagan sorcery
on its own terms.

The prominence of prophecy in the traditions of the
saints of Ireland and the Irish learning which was so
widely renowned throughout early Christian Europe
can only have been inherited from the druids. The Irish
monastic schools — most notable amongst them the
foundations of Finnian at Clonard and Enda on the
Aran islands, which together could claim to have
trained all the great saints of sixth-century Ireland —
were cast in the mould, and even founded on the sites,
of the druidic colleges. The oak tree and oak grove are
known, even from classical sources, to have been sacred
to the druids and it is no accident that the word *daire,*
the Irish name for the oak, is to be found in the ancient
names of so many great monastic churches, of which
Columcille's *Daire-magh,* "the field of the oaks," at
Durrow and Brigid's *Cill-Dara,* "the church of the oak,"
at Kildare are just two prominent examples. So numerous are the druidic aspects of the ancient Irish church
that it must have been through the druid that the Irish
holy man inherited a spiritual consciousness with its
roots deep in the Celtic, even the pre-Celtic, past.

Some number of cultural characteristics have long
been associated with the Celt and they are traits
shared in some measure by all Celtic peoples. Imagina-
tive, creative, fond of display on one hand, fickle and
war-proud on the other, the Celts have also been
recognized, even by Caesar and Livy in the first
century before Christ, as possessed of an extraordinary

and profound spirituality and that ancient testimony
has been confirmed by much more recent archaeology.

The archaeologist often chooses to identify each stage
in the development of a civilization by the place-name
of the site where it was first and most fully revealed.
Consequently, archaeology's first recognition of a fully-
formed Celtic presence in Europe is known as the
"Halstatt Culture" from the salt-mining township near
Salzburg in Austria, where the discovery of a great
wealth of iron-worked grave goods from the beginning
of the eighth century BC provided the archaeologist
with his landmark for the emergence of the warrior
Celt out of the Indo-European expansion into the river
valleys of central Europe. The ornamented iron bowls,
horse-trappings and wargear found in the graves of
Halstatt can only have been intended to furnish the
passage of the occupants of those graves into the realm
of the dead and, whatever else might be claimed for
Celtic spirituality, there can be nowhere any doubt that
these people emerged from the mists of prehistory
believing in a life after death.

# The legacy of Irish tradition

No pagan Celt bequeathed to posterity any account of
the beliefs which shaped his cosmos. All that is known
— and it is a very great deal — of the gods and heroes
of pre-Christian Ireland is preserved in manuscripts of
the eleventh and twelfth centuries which are derived,
if not transcribed, from texts set down as much as five
hundred years earlier.

The coming of Christianity to Ireland brought with
it the Latin alphabet to shape the Goidelic tongue into
the written language, now known as Old Irish, with

which Christian scribes fashioned cycles of myth and saga from the oral tradition of the bards. These early Irish myths and sagas represent a phenomenon unique to Ireland, sheltering a heritage which would have been condemned as pagan superstition elsewhere in the early Christian world and preserving within it a culture and cosmography of prehistoric antiquity. They have been described, by no less an authority on Celtic history and language than the late Professor Kenneth Jackson, as "a window on the Iron Age"[4] and confirm that the Irish Celts, in the way of other ancient peoples who translated ancestors and forbears into supernatural beings, created a mythic history from folk-memories of the gods and giants who walked the land before them. The prehistory of Ireland was thus presented as a series of "invasions of Erin," which can be shown, despite their being less than comfortably constrained within a biblical chronology, to correspond remarkably closely with the prehistoric cultures recognized by modern archaeology.

The mythology claims the first settlement of Ireland to have been that of the people of Cessair, who "lived by fishing and fowling" and who had died out before the Flood, with which the archaeologist is in substantial agreement when he identifies the earliest people in Ireland — and, indeed, along much of the western seaboard — as Mesolithic hunters and gatherers. The second and third invasions were accomplished by the peoples of Partholón and Nemed, each of whom would seem to represent stages in the Neolithic cultures identified by archaeology as those of the first farmers and the builders of the great megalithic tombs in the third and fourth millennia BC. The mythology tells how the people of Nemed were driven from Ireland by the *Fomoire,* sea-demons portrayed as monstrous spawn of

the Old Testament Cain and who appear not to have
invaded the land of Ireland but instead to have preyed
upon it from the sea. If these Fomoire represent a
mythologization of warrior tribes infesting the Outer
Hebrides, Orkney and Shetland in the second millennium BC, then they were kindred stock to the first of
the two "invasions of Erin" which represent the cultures of the Irish Bronze Age. These people were the
*Fir Bolg,* a mythic form of the culture known to the
archaeologist from their characteristic drinking cups as
the "Beaker People," who were superseded in their turn
by a later Bronze Age culture, possibly even the Indo-
European advance guard known as proto-Celts, but
identified in the mythology as the *Túatha Dé Danann.*

These "clans of the goddess Danu" were the last
settlement of Ireland before the arrival of the Goidelic
Celts and their mythic history forms the theme of the
legends which comprise the "Mythological" cycle. The
Túatha Dé Danann are portrayed as magical, even
godlike, beings who introduced learning, sorcery and
metalcraft to Ireland and were able to throw a barrier
of sea-mist around the island in an attempt to ward off
the last of the "invasions of Erin." In the event, the
Túatha Dé Danann were unable to throw back the
invasion of Ireland by the people of *Miledh* — clearly
recognizable as the mythic form of the Goidelic Celts —
and fled, by way of the tomb-mounds called the *sídh,*
into the otherworld from whence they emerge throughout the subsequent mythic history of Celtic Ireland.
The same thin veil separating the world of the living
from the otherworld of the ancient dead characterizes
Irish Celtic consciousness both before and after Christianity. There is an anecdote from the Patrick legend,
by way of illustration, which tells of the saint's encounter with a woman of the Túatha Dé Danann emerging

from the *sídh* with her youth and beauty entirely
unimpaired by the passing of at least a thousand years.

The deliberately ambiguous parentage of the legendary Irish kings seems always to imply their being
offspring of one of the Túatha Dé Danann and the
otherworld aspect of the warrior hero is ever-present in
the sagas of the "Ulster" and "Fenian" cycles. The
outstanding example is the mighty Cúchulainn, who
stands at the heroic centre of the Ulster Cycle and was
born the son of Lugh, the god-king of the Túatha Dé
Danann known as "The Shining One." The monastic
scribe placed the epic events of the Ulster Cycle in the
first century AD, and specifically around the lifetime of
Christ, but they are nonetheless wholly the property of
pagan Ireland. So too are the tales of Finn mac-Cumaill, hero of the Fenian Cycle, which are set in the
time of the historical king, Cormac mac-Airt, credited
by the annals with leading the first Irish raids on
Roman Britain in the early third century. Finn and his
warband, the *fian,* were élite fighting men, the first
professional soldiers recorded in Ireland, yet the sagas
tell of their familiar involvement with the people of the
*sídh* and identify Finn's own mother as of the Túatha
Dé Danann.

Finn mac-Cumaill is also a prime example of the
extent to which the Irish tradition mythologized not
only ancestors and forbears but also the very landscape
of Ireland. The basalt columns of the Giant's Causeway
on the Antrim coast — long associated with Finn in
recognition of the otherworld-aspected hero as necessarily of greater stature than mere mortal men — is
the most famous of countless sites not only in Ireland
but along the whole western seaboard marking the
traditional scene of Fenian adventurings. So too are the
feats of the warrior hero, Cúchulainn, associated with

innumerable sites in the north of Ireland, most especially the hillfort at Navan, known in the mythos as
Emain Macha, capital fortress of the ancient kingdom
of Ulster.

The interweaving of legend with landscape went still
deeper into the mythic past than the Celtic heroic age
and, while the ancient Irish tradition included no
creation myth, the collateral texts which supplement
the Mythological Cycle systematically attribute the
very shaping of the land to the peoples who settled
Ireland before the Celt. There were three lakes and
nine rivers in Erin when Partholón arrived after the
Flood. Seven more lakes appeared in his time, another
four in the time of Nemed and three more in the time
of the Túatha Dé Danann. Similarly, the clearing of the
land was attributed to the work of pre-Celtic peoples.
Partholón cleared four great plains and Nemed cleared
twelve — a proposal with which the modern archaeologist investigating Neolithic farming would be in sub-
stantive, if not precise, agreement. In much the same
sequence was the political division of Ireland accomplished in mythic antiquity, divided first by Partholón
into four provinces and finally into five by the Fir Bolg.
"And that" — according to the *Lebor Gabála Érenn,* the
ancient "Book of Invasions of Erin" — "is the division
of the provinces of Ireland which shall endure for ever."

For all its remarkable occasions of concurrence with
the prehistory of Ireland proposed by modern archaeological science, the "folk-history" preserved in Irish
tradition is, of course, still a mythologized account of
the past. The advent of each new prehistoric culture
did not drive the people of the antecedent settlement to
depart the land, as the "invasions of Erin" thesis claims
and, indeed, Celtic Ireland emerges into history as a

culture drawing on wellsprings from the Bronze Age
and before. The central importance here of the mythic
history of Ireland is the fact of its currency in the early
Christian period. The impact of the new faith appears
to have renewed rather than revolutionized the cosmography of the Irish Celt, and the Christian scribes who
transcribed the bardic tradition on to the manuscript
page presented it in terms of a natural and inevitable
progress of Celtic spirituality towards Christianity.
Neither, in so doing, were they necessarily guilty of any
great distortion, because the ambiguity of human and
divine in Christ the man-god surrounded by the
compelling humanity of his saints can only have held
a natural magnetism for a pre-Christian tradition
which had long found great significance in mysterious
conceptions and descent from the divine, wondrous
births and deaths foretold.

The cycles of myth and saga reveal the most ancient
surviving account of the world and world-view of Celtic
Ireland. The holy men of the ancient Irish church,
recognized as the most characteristically Celtic of
saints, were born of that same world and heirs to that
same world-view — and it is against that background
that their white martyrdom comes most sharply into
focus.

The holy man who sought the white martyrdom of
voluntary exile, "resolving to seek a foreign country for
the love of Christ,"[5] was dedicating himself to the
greater, even the ultimate, pursuit of the monastic
ideal. Not only was he choosing to separate himself
from every tie of clan and kinship, from the whole
complex pattern of blood-bond with tribe and ancestor
which formed the bedrock of his society and its culture,
but he was also taking himself away from the very land
of Ireland where every lake and river, every hill, plain

and promontory, had been named and known by
generations beyond recollection for its association with
the life or death of ancestors and ancients.

Such, then was the great significance of the white
martyrdom for the ancient Irish church and the association of the holy man with exile would seem to be as
old as the very earliest evidence for Christianity in
Ireland. In the opening lines of his *Letter to Coroticus,*
the oldest surviving document from the history of early
Christian Ireland, the historical Patrick declares
himself to be "an exile for the love of God." The significance of his remark might have been dismissed as no
more than coincidence, if only on the grounds of Patrick
having not been an Irish Celt, were it not for his own
admission of his conversion in Ireland and significant
allusions to pilgrimage and exile in the later sources
for at least two of the pre-Patrician saints of Ireland,
Ciaran of Saigir and Ailbe of Emly, both of whom are
invoked in the *Litany of Pilgrim Saints.*

By reason of Ireland's being an island in the ocean, the
Irish holy man's quest for the white martyrdom of exile
necessarily involved him in sea-voyage and it is in the
prehistorical, no less than the spiritual, significance of
the sea that the ancient Irish church shares so much
common ground with the spirituality of pre-Christian
Ireland.

The Pharisaic *Book of Enoch* from the second century
BC reflects the belief of many ancient peoples in its
description of the "kingdom of the dead" as "the eternal
west, the setting of all the suns." It was a belief shared
also by the Goidelic Celts who found themselves at the
edge of the sea beyond which the sun sank in the
distant west. When the holy man Columban, whose
quest for the white martyrdom led him to Gaul in the

last decade of the sixth century, described his own people to the Pope as "the Irish, dwellers at the ends of the earth," he was echoing a world-view which had been shared by his Celtic ancestors for at least a thousand years. For the prehistoric Gael looking out from the land of Ireland, the vast and trackless ocean he saw before him offered the way to "the eternal west, the setting of all the suns" beyond which lay the otherworld which he knew as *Tír na n-Og*, "the land of the ever-young."

The sea as the way to the otherworld was the domain of Manannan, the god-king of the Túatha Dé Danann surnamed *mac-Lir* or "son of the sea," who rides through the mythos as "the horseman of the maned sea," his sword the lightning of the storm, and his armour the sea-mist around the shores of Erin. Manannan personifies the sea in all its moods and he confirms how deep an impression was made on the Celtic imagination by the sea-roads which had brought them to the western edge of the world. For the Roman, the sea presented a barrier to the advance of the legions, but for the Celt, as for the prehistoric peoples who had gone before him, the ocean was his great thoroughfare of migration and communication and so it was for the Celtic holy man of the ancient Irish church whose quest for the white martyrdom led him, in the event almost inevitably, along the sea-road to the Hebrides.

# Celtic Scotland

It is often said, and it cannot be said too often, that "the past is a foreign country." Nowhere is that more true than in the region of north Britain which has been

known for less than a thousand years as Scotland. The
name itself is of the greatest significance for the period
under consideration here, because it derives from that
by which the Romans called the sea-raiders out of the
north of Ireland who preyed on *provincia Britannica* in
the days of Empire, the *Scotti* or "Scots."

The formal history of the settlement of these "Irish
in Britain" begins within a decade of the death of the
historical Patrick and there were — at least officially
— no "Scots" in what is now "Scotland" until the end of
the fifth century AD. Before that time and through the
centuries of Roman Britain, the lands to the north of
Hadrian's Wall were the domain, as was Ireland, of
Celtic peoples, but peoples who were distinctly unlike
the Irish in terms of their culture, history and form of
language.

The tribes whose territory lay between the firths of
Forth and Clyde were Britons speaking the Britonic
form of Celtic language, whose culture had been re-
shaped over four hundred years of Roman influence.
The Britons in the west were the tribe of the Damnonii,
whose kingdom of Strathclyde was centred on their
capital fortress on Dumbarton Rock, which name
derives from "the Dun of the Britons." They had been,
at least nominally, Christian since the early fourth
century when the new faith was adopted as the religion
of the Empire under Constantine the Great and, even
though Patrick's letter to their king Ceretic suggests
that their Christian integrity had been defrayed by a
reversion to tribalism which followed the withdrawal of
the imperial administration, the kingdom on the Clyde
represented the resolutely Christian bastion of Britonic
power in the north and a barrier to the northern
expansion of pagan Anglo-Saxon Northumbria through
the sixth century.

North of the Forth-Clyde line and into the highlands and islands, the political, cultural and ethnographic geography becomes much less distinct. The peoples of the further north are called, for reasons of essentially historical convenience, the Picts from the name first applied to them by the Romans in the later third century. They were, in all probability, a fusion of the descendants of aboriginal peoples of the Bronze Age and earlier with an overlay of Britonic-derived Celtic warrior aristocracy. Their language — or, more probably, languages — remains a subject of scholarly speculation, although it is believed to have been a form of Britonic-Celtic which possibly retained elements surviving from pre-Indo-European tongues. Scattered across the vast and inaccessible landscape of the highlands and islands, these "Pictish" tribes were effectively independent of any central authority and appear to have come only occasionally under the aegis of a high-king until the later seventh century, but on those occasions they presented a ferocious military opposition to a centuries-long sequence of Roman, Irish, and northern English enemies.

Such, then, were the peoples of Scotland before the historical settlement of the Scots which is formally dated by the Irish annalists to the year 498 when the royal princes of the Irish kingdom of Dalriada, whose territory lay in what is now Antrim, crossed the North Channel to claim the mainland and islands between the Mull of Kintyre and the Firth of Lorn as their new kingdom of Scotic Dalriada. There is, in fact, evidence in the legendary history of the Irish to indicate the earlier presence of an Irish settlement on Kintyre and the surrounding territory, very probably with sufficiently strong links of kinship and allegiance to Irish Dalriada to legitimize the Dalriadic royal house as its overlords.

The Irish had been attempting to colonize the
western periphery of Roman Britain since the fourth
century — unsuccessfully in north Wales where they
were driven out of Gwynedd but with more success to
the south in Dyfed and, possibly also, Devon and
Cornwall — and the first serious settlements in the
west of Scotland would have most probably been
attempted at around the same time. However early it
had begun, the Irish settlement of the west of Scotland
was firmly established by the first decade of the sixth
century and in the wake of the colonists and their
kings out of Ireland came the holy men of the ancient
Irish church.

It may not have been entirely accidental that this
settlement of Scotic Dalriada was almost precisely
contemporary with the very earliest evidence for the
pursuit of the white martyrdom of exile by the saints
of Ireland. The holy men who chose voluntary exile
from clan, kindred and homeland were, after all,
choosing the white rather than the red martyrdom and
there was virtually nowhere else outside of Ireland
where exile could be attempted with any degree of
safety. The mainland of Britain south of the Clyde was
under ever greater pressure from the aggressive
expansion of the pagan Germanic settlement and it
would be at least another fifty years before it became
possible to journey in any great confidence of safety
along the sea-road to Gaul and the continent.

Scotic Dalriada, by contrast, offered the ideal prospect for the saint in search of the white martyrdom.
The mainland of Scotland was known in the contemporary Irish sources, even until the early eighth century,
as "the land of Britain," and afterwards called by the
Irish name of Alba. So too were the isles of the Hebrides which lay along its western seaboard called "the

islands of Britain" and the settlement of Scotic Dalriada, similarly, as "the Irish in Britain." It was thus made possible for an Irish holy man to seek "a foreign country for the love of Christ" and still enjoy the protection of a Christian Irish king of an Irish kingdom beyond the land of Ireland.

Neither was the greater extent of the western seaboard unknown territory to the mythic prehistory preserved in Irish tradition. The sagas tell how the young Cúchulainn learned his skill with the sword from a giantess on Skye and Finn mac-Cumaill's adventuring throughout the Hebrides is commemorated in numerous places, most famous of them all being Fingal's Cave on Staffa. In still more distant mythic history, one of the three clans of the people of Nemed driven from Ireland by the predatory Fomoire found their way — by implication along the sea-road to the otherworld — to the north of Alba from whence they returned to Ireland transformed into the magical Túatha Dé Danann. On their return they overcame the Fir Bolg, who had settled the land in their absence, and drove them out of Ireland to find refuge on Rathlin Island (anciently included as one of the Hebrides), Arran, Islay and the Innsegall, by which name the medieval Irish called the Western Isles.

Thus the ancient Irish tradition records — and, it would seem, with remarkable accuracy — the prehistory of the Hebrides, which name, incidentally, is of very much greater antiquity than the name of Scotland. The geographer Ptolemy was just one of the classical authors who knew from the voyages of Pytheas in the third century BC of islands north of Ireland called Eboudai, a name of probably pre-Celtic origin long since corrupted into the modern form of "Hebrides." Through the period of the Neolithic and the Bronze Age

which followed it, the islands of the western sea were
settled in turn by a sequence of cultures whose archi-
tects in sea, sky and stone raised the megalithic
masterwork at Callanish on the Isle of Lewis. The
Callanish stone circle and its attendant stone rows are
believed now to have been raised as a lunar calendar of
the seasons and by a seafaring people who recognized
the influence of the moon on the tides. Whatever other
characteristics archaeology might reveal about these
cultures, they were beyond any doubt peoples of such
maritime accomplishment as to enable the eminent
prehistorian V. Gordon Childe to propose "the grey
waters of the Irish Sea [and, by inference, of the entire
western seaboard] as bright with Neolithic argonauts
as the Western Pacific is today."[6]

# Sea-road of the Saints

Celtic Ireland was a society still informed by the
cultures of its Neolithic and Bronze Age past and,
consequently, heir to their knowledge and experience of
the western sea. The curragh with its hull of tarred
calico stretched over a wooden frame, which is still to
be found in the west of Ireland, is, in all essentials, the
same craft as the skin-boat used by those prehistoric
seafarers. In the way of the ironies of history, it was in
just such a craft, called a *curach* in the early sources,
that the slave-raiders who carried Patricius into
captivity in Ireland crossed the Irish Sea and the holy
man Columcille made his first landfall — in the place
since known as *Port a Curraich,* "the Bay of the
Curach" — on Iona.

   The Atlantic seaboard of Ireland and Scotland,
"where these vessels could be readily run ashore in

some sheltered bay or cove and hauled up above the high-water mark," has been described as "a curach coast" and the ocean-going curach — its hide hull stretched over a wooden frame some ten metres long and driven by sail or oar — has been recognized as "one of the most significant products of the ancient civilization of the Gael."[7]

The curach, which will be the subject of some further attention in these pages, was a craft which might have been designed by prehistory for the sea-road of the saints, because there can be no doubt that it was the maritime tradition of the prehistoric peoples of the western seaways, preserved by the Irish through at least two thousand years, which made possible the great pilgrimage of the Celtic holy man out of Ireland in search of the white martyrdom of exile, through the islands of the Hebrides to seek out his hermitage in the ocean, and on into the north Atlantic — in the great act of faith of the ancient Irish church — to find the Christian otherworld of the "Land of Promise of the Saints."

# KINTYRE
# "A Grey Eye upon Erin"

There are some place-names which reward even the most casual investigation of their antiquity and etymology with an especial insight into the past and Kintyre is one of them. The modern form of an Irish name at least as old as the seventh century and in all probability very much older, it derives from the Gaelic *ceann-tír,* quite literally "headland," and is a clear reflection of the Irish perspective on the Kintyre peninsula as the southernmost prominence of what is now Scotland.

The Mull of Kintyre lies no more than thirteen miles distant from Fair Head on the coast of Antrim and, when seafaring within sight of land was the customary preference of the most ancient navigators, there can

have been no time in the past when that shortest sea-
crossing between the two countries represented any
kind of barrier to peoples of a maritime inclination.
Like giant stepping stones into the ocean, the island
chain of Islay and Jura and the headland of Kintyre
had beckoned the Bronze Age seafarers remembered in
Irish tradition as the Fir Bolg and, two thousand years
after them, the princes of Dalriada who were to lay the
first foundations of the kingdom of the Scots.

In the wake of warlords seeking sword-land came the
holy men in quest of the white martyrdom, for whom
even the short voyage across the North Channel
represented a passage of great spiritual significance. If
not the first — and there can be no doubt that he was
not the first Irish holy man to cross into Scotland —
then assuredly the foremost amongst them was the
saint who is still known to the sea-divided Gael by his
Celtic name of Columcille, from the Irish *Colum Cille*
or "Colum of the Church," but now most widely called
by his Latin name-form of *Columba*.

# Columba's "pilgrimage to Britain"

At Keil Point near the village of Southend around the
eastern flank of the Mull of Kintyre, a slab of rock
bears the impression of two footprints which tradition
insists to have been left there by St Columba's first
setting foot in Scotland, but which might here provide
a salutary index of the extent to which the historical St
Columba has been no better served by tradition than
the historical St Patrick before him.

While a local stonemason admitted — in the course
of his deathbed confession in the year 1864 — to
having cut the second footprint with his own mischie-

vous hand, its companion impression is of very much greater antiquity and was almost certainly already carved in that rock long before Columba left Ireland. It is one of a number of similar rock-cut footprints, survivals from the Iron Age found elsewhere in western Scotland and also in Ireland, which are believed to have served some ritual purpose most probably associated with the proclamation of kings. While the tradition of "Columba's Footprints" is blatantly apocryphal, it does, like much else in the canon of Columban tradition, contain a kernel of genuine historical plausibility, because the destination of the saint's voyage from Ireland was, without any doubt, the peninsula of Kintyre.

The story which still enjoys an unfortunately wide popular currency — telling of the "St Columba" who was driven into exile as penance for causing a battle to be fought in defence of his making an illicit copy of a psalter, who came to the island of Iona as the first landfall from where he could no longer see Ireland in the distance, and there founded his missionary base for the conversion of the same number of souls lost in battle — is an anachronistic conflation of medieval legends, serving to distort whatever genuine traditions they might otherwise preserve and doing the very least justice to the extraordinary man revealed by the early sources as the historical Columba. Pre-eminent among those sources is the most ancient and authoritative surviving *Life* of the saint, written less than a hundred years after his death by his kinsman and successor abbot of Iona, Adamnan.

Unusually among the *Lives* of Irish saints — almost all of them found only in medieval manuscripts and most of them, whilst deriving from more ancient

sources, the work of medieval authors — Adamnan's
*Vita Columbae* (written in Latin and thus initiating the
use of the Latin name-form) is preserved in a manuscript set down, if not during its author's lifetime then
certainly within a decade of his death. Its provenance
is beyond dispute and so, indeed — on the evidence of
its author's own preface — is that of its sources in
reflecting the monastic tradition of Iona almost within
living memory of its founding saint.

> Let no one think of me as either stating what
> is not true regarding so great a man, or record-
> ing anything doubtful or uncertain. Let him
> know that I will tell with all candour, and with-
> out any ambiguity, what I have learned from the
> consistent narrative of my predecessors, trust-
> worthy and discerning men, and that my narra-
> tive is founded either on written authorities
> anterior to my own times, or on what I have
> myself heard from some learned and faithful
> ancients, unhesitatingly attesting facts, the
> truth of which they had themselves diligently
> inquired into.

Nowhere in Adamnan — nor, for that matter, in the
second oldest surviving *Life,* the Irish *Betha Colaim
Chille,* set down in Derry in the twelfth century — is
there to be found any reference to Columba being
banished from Ireland. While he does weave a wealth
of biographical and historical detail into his *Life of
Columba,* Adamnan disregards any attempt at biographical narrative to concentrate on prophecies,
miracles and visions as the expression of the exemplary
holiness of his saint. Only in his second preface does he
offer even the most summary biography and deals with

Columba's momentous pilgrimage out of Ireland in a single sentence.

> In the second year after the battle of Cul-
> drevny [fought in AD 561], and in the forty-sec-
> ond year of his age, Columba, resolving to seek a
> foreign country for the love of Christ, sailed from
> Ireland to Britain.

For all his brevity, Adamnan — who was writing at the same time as the Iona scribes compiling the chronicle which formed the basis of the later Irish annals and using the Irish annalist's device of dating events in relation to battles — does confirm the date of Columba's birth as 521 and of his pilgrimage out of Ireland as the year 563. He is also quite unequivocal in presenting its great purpose as the quest for the white martyrdom of voluntary exile.

A contrasting account of the same event, written some eight hundred and fifty years after that of Adamnan and at far greater length, is set down in the collection of Columban tradition compiled under the title *Betha Colaim Chille* ("Life of Columcille") by Manus O'Donnell, son of the Lord of Tirconnell, in 1532. Writing in an idiom which has more in common with the sagas of Finn and Cúchulainn than the monastic world of Adamnan, O'Donnell collected together into biographical form the wealth of folklore which had built up around the saint in his own clan country of Derry and Donegal over a thousand years and, in so doing, provided the principal source of material since recast into the spurious popular legend of "St Columba." The story of the saint's illicit tran-scription of a manuscript has its origins in a medieval legend intended to link the historical battle of Culdrev-

ny with the psalter, known as the *Cathach* or "Battler,"
enshrined in a golden case and long believed to be in
Columba's own hand, which had been prized by the
O'Donnells since the eleventh century as a talisman of
triumph in war. While many of the tales included in
the *Betha Colaim Chille* can be shown to have a similar
provenance, there are others which may well preserve
elements from more genuinely ancient tradition.

One such is the account — rich in local detail and
illustrated with bardic quatrains ascribed to Columcille
himself — of the saint's taking his leave of Ireland. It
describes his tribal kinsfolk "lamenting on this side and
that of Lough Foyle," his bidding farewell to "Derry of
the Oaks" where he had founded his first monastery
some twenty years earlier, and the course of his curach
"through Lough Foyle to the place where the lake
entered into the great sea...on the path to beetling-
browed Alba."

And he bade farewell to Erin then, and they
put out into the ocean and the great deep. And
Columcille kept gazing backward on Erin till the
sea hid it from him.... And it was thus he made
the quatrain below:

"I stretch my eye across the brine,
From the firm oaken planks;
Many the tears of my soft grey eye
As I look back upon Erin.

There is a grey eye
That will look back upon Erin;
Never again will it see
The men or women of Erin..."

The narrative of the twelfth-century Irish *Life* passes directly on from Columba's departure from Ireland to his arrival on Iona and would seem to have been Manus O'Donnell's authority for his statement that "history telleth no more of him until he came to the isle called I-Columcille," but the much older and more historically reliable evidence of Adamnan, for all that it offers no precise location for Columba's first setting foot in Scotland, does point indisputably to a landfall on Kintyre.

Adamnan's reference to *caput regionis,* or "headland," is a direct translation into Latin of the Irish *ceann-tír,* and corresponds convincingly to the place and prospect evoked by the bardic phrase "beetling-browed Alba" quoted by O'Donnell. Columba might well have first landed in one of the bays around the Mull of Kintyre. He might, no less probably, have found his curach carried further up the west coast of Kintyre by the current and into the inlet of Loch Caolisport, where a natural cavern above a bay on its north-west shore is known as "Columba's Cave." Tradition again, admittedly, but a tradition very much more credible than "Columba's Footprints."

Caves have been long and often associated with Celtic holy men, perhaps representing naturally-formed places of retreat from the world, but perhaps also representing a legacy of pre-Christian druidic practices. Megalithic tombs, recognized in Celtic Ireland as points of entry to the otherworld of the *sídh,* were usually called "caves" in the Irish sources and at least one of the saints of Ireland — Coemgen of Glendalough — chose as his first hermitage a Bronze Age tomb in the Wicklow mountains. "Columba's Cave" — with a cross of the most ancient *Chi-Rho* form carved into the rock wall above a primitive stone altar — had been used, on

the evidence of excavated stone coffins, for early
Christian burials and was certainly a holy place at
much the same time as Columba's arrival in Scotland.
If that arrival had been along the shore of Loch Caolisport, it would have brought the saint much closer to his
intended destination, because while the white martyrdom of exile is presented as his great spiritual purpose,
the place of that exile was directed by more urgently
temporal concerns.

The earliest recorded date for Columba's foundation
on Iona is entered by the eighth-century Northumbrian
historian, Bede, as the year 565, two years after
Adamnan's date for his voyage from Ireland, and there
is every likelihood that Iona was not even his first
monastic foundation in Scotland. The real destination
of the historical St Columba in the year 563 was not
the holy island of Iona, but the hillfort at Dunadd,
capital fortress of his kinsmen, the high-kings of Scotic
Dalriada.

# The kingdom of Dalriada

Dunadd — from the Gaelic *Dùn Ad,* "fortress on the
Add" — is the most impressively preserved of the
hillfort sites which stood as the great symbols of power
in ancient Celtic Scotland. An isolated prominence
rising up out of the Crinan Moss and overlooking the
river Add from which it took its name, entirely secure
from any surprise attack and all but the most deter-
mined attempt at siege, Dunadd must have appeared
as the outstanding natural stronghold of Iron Age
Argyll. The hillfort today represents the result of a
sequence of phases of occupation, each of them taking
advantage of the defensive landform, which may have

begun as early as the pre-Celtic Bronze Age with a small fort on the western summit around which were added extensive ramparts to complete the fortress of the Dalriadic Scots still in use through the eighth century AD.

The outstanding defensive qualities of Dunadd and its access, by way of the river Add into Loch Crinan, to the sea would have been a great magnet to any Dark Age warlord, but an Irish Celt would have been no less attracted by its immediate proximity to what has been called the "ritual landscape"[8] of the Kilmartin valley, where the most remarkable concentration of prehistoric rock-carved art in Scotland is still to be found on the stone slabs, cairns, and circles left by the megalithic cultures of the second and third millennia BC. Much as the megalithic tombs of the Boyne valley in Ireland made so great and enduring an impression on the Celtic imagination that the same spirals and rhomboids carved on their stones thousands of years before Christ found their way on to high crosses and gospel book pages as characteristic motifs of Celtic Christian art, so the Irish Celtic warlords who claimed Dunadd as their capital fortress would have recognized the cup, ring and spiral carvings on cairns and circles already some three thousand years old as the legacy of gods and giants out of their own ancient myths and sagas.

The beginnings of the kingdom of Scotic Dalriada lie across the threshold over which history emerges out of legend and the tradition of the "three sons of Erc" — Fergus, Oengus and Loarn — who left their father's kingdom in Antrim to claim territories of their own along the west coast of Scotland, has been shown to be a legendary contrivance which does not occur in the sources before the tenth century. It is, nonetheless, only two-thirds legend, because the first of the three

names does represent the genuinely historical founder
of the royal dynasty of Scotic Dalriada, *Fergus Mór
mac-Erc* ("Fergus the Great, Erc's son"), whose obituary
was entered at the year 501 by the *Annals of Tigernach.*

> Fergus Mór mac-Erc, with the people of Dalri-
> ada, held part of Britain; and there he died.

An Irish tradition, known to Bede and accepted by him
as historical, tells how the dynast Cairbre Riada, who
had led his people of the Dal Riata out of famine-
stricken Munster to establish the original kingdom of
Dalriada in Antrim around AD 200, had afterwards
established a colony "north of the Clyde," probably in
Cowal, in the third century. There are similar legends
elsewhere in the mythic history, which leave no doubt
that there had been Irish settlements established in
Scotland for possibly as long as two hundred years
before the arrival of Fergus mac-Erc and, against that
background, Oengus and Loarn are to be most realistically recognized, not as "sons of Erc," but as the
eponymous forbears of the Cenél nOengussa on Islay
and the Cenél Loairn around Oban who have been
convincingly identified by Professor Archie Duncan as
"ruling kindreds from an earlier migration of Dal Riata
to Scotland"[9] who acknowledged Fergus Mór as their
over-king in the last years of the fifth century.

The various dates entered in the earliest sources for
the foundation of the kingdom of Dalriada in Scotland
are confused almost beyond hope of precise resolution,
but they can be taken to indicate the arrival of Fergus
and his warband on Kintyre in the last years of the
fifth century. The year 498 entered by the *Annals of
Clonmacnois* is as plausible as any other, and taken

with Tigernach's date of 501 for Fergus' death, would indicate his reign in Scotland as of brief duration, even by Dark Age standards. His son and successor Domangart outlived his father by just six years, before the succession passed, in turn, to his sons Comgall and Gabran, for whom were named the *cenéla* Comgaill and Gabráin, the two royal clans of Scotic Dalriada.

Through the six decades which separate the death of Fergus Mór from the arrival of the holy man Columba, the fortunes of the kingdom of Scotic Dalriada veered from early expansion to dramatic decline. After the short reigns of Fergus and Domangart, the succession of Comgall in 507 and that of his brother Gabran in 538 marked a period of Dalriadic expansion sufficient to alarm the Pictish tribes whose territories lay to the east and north. The Picts — whose language has been barely identified, far less translated — left no documentary record of their own past and, in consequence, such Pictish history as has survived has been pieced together from the sources set down by other cultures who came into, usually hostile, contact with them. Even on the evidence of so fragmentary a history, it would seem that the Picts were fearsome warriors who presented the most serious military threat when their tribes were brought into alliance under a single supreme warlord, and it was Gabran's great misfortune to rule Dalriada in the time of Bruide mac-Maelchon's ascendancy as high-king of Picts. The entry in the *Annals of Tigernach* at the year 560 is a characteristically terse Irish annalist's record of the events which had brought Scotic Dalriada to the edge of disaster.

Death of Gabran, son of Domangart, king of Alba.
Flight of the Scots before Bruide, son of
       Maelchon, king of Picts.

While the early sources preserve no further details
of the "flight of the Scots before Bruide" and neither
do they indicate whether or not Gabran was a casualty
of the conflict — although the coincidence of the
two events can be taken to imply that he must have
been — they do indicate Scotic Dalriada being made
tributary to the high-king of Picts as the price of
peace following a crushing defeat. Gabran is acknowledged by the annals as *rí Albain* — which
translates as "king of Alba," even if it actually meant
"king in Alba" — but his nephew and successor, Conall
mac-Comgall, is described only as *rí Dalriada,* suggesting that while he remained king of Dalriada in Ireland
he could no longer claim the stature of kingship in
Scotland.

For all their fragmentary account of events, the early
sources leave nowhere any doubt that the kingdom of
the "Irish in Britain" entered the decade of the 560s
with its fortunes at their lowest ebb, even with its very
survival under threat, and it is against just such a
political backdrop that the arrival of Columba can be
set into its most historical context.

# The historical St Columba

The summary biography included in the second preface
to Adamnan's *Life of Columba* makes only the most
modest reference to the saint's being "born of noble
parents" and names his father as Feidlimid mac-
Fergus. The true stature of the saint's lineage is
revealed by the genealogy of his grandfather Fergus
Cendfota, who was the son of Conall Gulban and the
grandson of Niall Noígiallach, Niall of the Nine Hostages, legendary king of all Ireland in the last quarter

of the fourth century and dynast of the Uí Neill, the royal "race of Niall."

The son of Feidlimid who was born at Gartan in the "waterfall land" of Donegal in the year 521, who forsook his given name of Crimthan for the monastic name of Colum Cille and passed into history as "St Columba" was, in fact, a prince of the blood royal of the Cenél Conaill, the clan of Conall, son of Niall. Finnian of Clonard, teacher to very many of the great saints of Ireland, is said to have chided his humbly-born pupil, the future St Ciaran of Clonmacnois, by reminding him that while he had abandoned only the birthright of a carpenter's son for a monastic calling, his friend Columcille had renounced his rightful claim on the high-kingship of Ireland for the church.

The portrait of Columba which emerges out of even the most ancient and authoritative sources is one of a man of sudden contrasts, by turns seer and scribe, consort of angels and counsellor of kings, almost as if its outlines are diffused by the constantly changing light of the islands where crisp profiles dissolve in moments and grey distances reappear as a radiant reflection of sunlight after rain. For all the authority of Adamnan's claim that "while dwelling on earth he appeared to live like the saints of Heaven," the *Life of Columba* reveals a holy man with the blood of the warlord Niall coursing through his veins and for whom the claim of the *túath* could never be denied.

The battle of Culdrevny — of which spurious later tradition claims Columba to have been the cause — was fought by Columba's own people of the northern Uí Neill in alliance with the king of Connaught against the high-king Diarmait mac-Cerbaill of the rival southern branch of the Uí Neill, and the saint's loyalties in the contest can have been in no doubt. The most

reliable historical record of the victory won by the host
of the northern Uí Neill and Connachta is the entry in
the *Annals of Ulster* which concludes with the statement that "through the prayers of Columcille they
conquered." Some similar political imperative inspired
by blood-kinship must also have prompted his pilgrimage to Britain, because while his male forbears had
been of the line of Niall, his father's mother was born
the niece of Fergus Mór mac-Erc and so the saint was
blood-kin to the royal house of Dalriada as well as the
Uí Neill.

All of which must be placed in the context of the
relationship between warlord and holy man which was
central to the introduction and establishment of
Christianity in a society structured on the tribal
warband. The process of conversion — following a
largely uniform pattern throughout Dark Age Britain
equally apparent in the evidence for Patricius in the
north of Ireland as in that for Augustine's missionary
Paulinus in Northumbria more than a hundred years
later — consisted of a direct approach to the warrior
king whose baptism into the new faith was followed, as
a matter of course, by its formal recognition throughout
his territories. None of which would demand that the
king, still less his people, abandoned their ancient
belief systems centred around omens and totems
reflecting the cycle of seasons, myths of tribal origin
and the otherworld of the ancestral dead on first
recognition of Christ the man-god. The old beliefs and
the new faith were never of necessity mutually exclusive,
and became, inevitably with the passage of time,
interwoven into the spiritual knotwork recognized in
retrospect as "Celtic Christianity."

When expressed in its most primitive form, the
initial encounter of the tribal warband society with

Christ the man-god consisted of the warlord being presented with a superior form of magic and convinced — if needs be by practical demonstration in wonder-working contests with the established pagan priesthood — of its potential to enhance the military glory upon which his authority ultimately depended, thus connecting the Christian *drui* to the ruling élite from their very first contact. So it was that the arrival in Scotic Dalriada in 563 of the holy man whose prayers had been so recently accredited with the defeat of a high-king of Ireland provided a kingdom suffering the consequences of its own, still more devastating, defeat with a magical figure whose charisma signified hope of restored fortunes. It was, in the event, a hope well-placed in a man of extraordinary qualities.

While the chronology of Adamnan's *Life* is never any better than vague, all the other evidence for the sequence of events would confirm his diplomatic mission to Bruide, king of Picts, as an early priority in Columba's activities in Scotland. The saint certainly visited Bruide in his fortress near Inverness before the foundation of his own monastery on Iona and Adamnan devotes a number of chapters to accounts of their meeting. While the Irish annals are in no doubt that it was "Conall, son of Comgall...who granted the island of Ia (Iona) to Columcille," Bede asserts that the Pictish king "gave him possession of the island" and neither statement need contradict the other when it would have been a necessary protocol for an over-king to sanction a gift of land by a tributary ruler.

The point on which Bede does disagree with the evidence of Adamnan is in his claim that Columba "converted the [Pictish] people to the Christian faith" and the entirely unhistorical tradition of Columba as the "Apostle of the Picts" has been shown to originate

with Bede's *Ecclesiastical History*. It is a work which
makes no secret of its author's great sympathy for the
Irish church, but was almost a century and a half after
Columba's time and from the perspective of the quite
different English Augustinian tradition. The northern
English church historian would seem to have misinter-
preted Columba's journey into Pictland as a Celtic
counterpart of Augustine's mission to Anglo-Saxon
England and ascribed to it the same purpose of conversion of a pagan people to Christianity, but there is no
evidence in Adamnan or any other early Irish source
for that being the case. Missionary purpose was never
any part of the white martyrdom in the ancient Irish
church and the "pilgrimage for Christ" was undertaken
into a "foreign country" which was always, even if only
nominally, Christian. There were certainly monks of
Iona in Pictish territories before the beginning of the
eighth century, but there is no record of any Columban
monastery in Pictland during the saint's lifetime, no
accounts of mass baptisms of Picts such as Bede
describes Paulinus conducting in Northumbria and
neither does Adamnan indicate the personal conversion
of Bruide — claiming only that the king "held this
reverend and holy man in very great honour."

Columba's mission into Bruide's kingdom was of a
diplomatic rather than evangelical nature and, on all
the evidence, fully accomplished its purpose. He was
able to negotiate securities from the king of Picts, not
only for the Irish church, but also for the kingdom of
the "Irish in Britain." It is certainly no accident that
Aidan mac-Gabran, the king appointed by the saint to
succeed on the death of Conall, "king of Dalriada," was
himself entered in the annals as *rí Albain*. Whether or
not Columba's noble lineage was the source of his
evident political instincts, it assuredly made a decisive

contribution to his eminence as a holy man and, by extension, to that of Iona as the mother church of a monastic *paruchia* which extended — even in the saint's own lifetime — from Tiree in the Hebrides to Durrow south-west of Ireland's ancient royal capital at Tara. When the high peak of the stature of a holy man in Celtic Ireland was his recognition as the patron saint of the *túath,* Columba was high-priest to both the Uí Neill and Cenél Gabráin and his foundation on Iona, thus, the church of the royal houses in two kingdoms. Foremost, then, among the Celtic holy men in the Hebrides, it can only have been Columba who inspired the ideal of the white martyrdom in the *Cambrai Homily,* but he was, in fact, following in a tradition as old as the earliest evidence for Irish Christianity.

# The pilgrimage of Ciaran of Saigir

It is the evidence for the pilgrimage of Ciaran of Saigir, anciently revered as the "first-born of the saints of Ireland," which confirms the sea-road of the saints to have been a part of the earliest Irish Christian tradition.

The first churches, hermitages and monasteries of the Irish church were built of wood, wattle and turf, materials so vulnerable to the erosion of almost fifteen hundred years as to have left almost no visible trace of their presence, but the evidence preserved in the form of place-names has proved very much more durable. Unlike the medieval and later custom of dedicating churches to biblical saints, the most ancient place-name dedications in the Celtic west commemorate the historical presence of holy men. Almost all those names incorporating a "Kil-" prefix which are found throughout Ireland and the west of Scotland can be taken to indicate the site of a *cill* or "cell," the place where one of the *peregrini* of the ancient Irish church had built his hermitage. As disciples were attracted to join him, his cell became the centre of an assembly of similar retreats which grew over time into a monastery. By then, it would seem, the founding saint had moved on, leaving his community in the care of a close companion, to renew his search for ever more remote withdrawal from the world and perhaps establishing more communities in the process, until he came to his destined "place of resurrection" where his tomb became the focus of miracles accredited to his name and a shrine for pilgrims thereafter. Similarly, other cell-sites along the route of his travels came to be regarded as holy places, sanctified ground chosen by local people as their place of burial. Even when the monastery which had grown up around the original cell was abandoned or destroyed, later secular settlements on the same site adopted, and often still retain, a place-name identifiable by its "Kil-" component as marking out a site of ancient sanctity. So too, other natural features, such as hills, lochs and, especially, wells, associated with some event in the life of a holy man came to be named for him. The distribution of genuine place-name dedications can, very often, serve to chart the travels and areas of activity of a saint and such is the evidence, taken together with fragments from the early sources, for Ciaran on Kintyre and, also, on Islay.

The greatest concentration of Ciaran place-names is found on Kintyre between Tarbert and Campbeltown, which was anciently called *Ceann Loch Cille Chiaráin,* the "the head of loch Kil-Ciaran," and its surrounding parish also formerly known as *Kilkerran*. There is another Loch Ciaran higher up the peninsula towards

Tarbert and another Kilchiaran parish across the sound on the island of Islay. It is unfortunate that these dedications have been attributed on occasion to another and more famous Ciaran, the abbot of Clonmacnois who died at the age of only thirty-three shortly after founding his great monastery on the Shannon in 545 and is nowhere recorded as having ever left Ireland.

Most of what is known of the historical Ciaran of Saigir — who is called *Sean-Ciarán,* or "Old Ciaran," in the Irish sources to distinguish him from the younger saint of Clonmacnois — has been compiled from fragments found in the *Martyrology of Oengus* and the *Litany of Pilgrim Saints,* both of which are now dated to around AD 800. His surviving *Lives* are medieval recensions of a much more ancient original, written within living memory of the saint but long since lost, and the value of their evidence is greatly distorted by the impact of the Patrick legend on the genuine traditions of the elder saints of Ireland.

The date of Ciaran's festival — the day of the year on which the church celebrates his ascent into Heaven — is entered in the Irish calendars on March 5th and, while the year of his death is nowhere recorded, he can be securely placed in the second half of the fifth century on the evidence of the Collect for his feast which begins by praising God for having "sent Ciaran into Ireland before any other saint" and a note in the *Martyrology of Oengus* which places his foundation of Saigir "thirty years before Patrick." He was born on Clear Island off the coast of Cork, the southernmost point of Ireland and lying close to the ancient sea-road from Gaul, but his principal foundation at Saigir (now Seirkieran, near Birr in County Offaly) lay in the territory of his father's people, the

Osraige, and became the royal burial-ground of the
kings of Ossory. His mother's clan were the Corcu
Loegde, who are named by the note in Oengus' calendar as the people among whom "the Cross was believed
in first in Ireland," a tradition which would well
correspond with Ciaran's stature as one of the elder
saints "before Patrick."

The authority of his tradition, already long-established by the end of the eighth century, would seem to
have presented a formidable obstacle to the scribes at
Armagh engaged in promoting the legend of Patrick as
the "Apostle of Ireland" and re-inventing other pre-
Patrician holy men as disciple-bishops ordained by
Patrick as his delegate missionaries. Ciaran was, by
then, so revered as an elder saint as to necessitate the
invention of his own custom-made diversion within the
Patrick legend. It took the form of having Ciaran make
a pilgrimage to Rome while Patrick was in Gaul
already intending his own return to Ireland, thereby
arranging for their paths to cross. The first chapter of
the Latin *Life of Ciaran* records Patrick's instructing
the saint as his delegate bishop.

> "Go before me to Ireland, and arrange a place
> for thyself in the middle of the island; and there
> shall be thy honour and thy resurrection."

A tale splendidly contrived for all its implausibility and
usefully facilitated by two elements already contained
within the Ciaran tradition. The first of these would
seem to be the "wild man" aspect attributed to Ciaran,
which cast him conveniently into the role of an Irish
"John the Baptist" preparing the way of the Apostle,
and portrayed him as clad in skins and living in caves
with wild creatures as his companions.

The association of Celtic holy men with wildlife occurs with great frequency throughout the early sources and can be traced back into prehistory when wild birds and animals represented tribal totems for the Irish Celt, but the tone of the beast and saint episodes in the Latin *Life of Ciaran* has an appealing quality all of its own. When Ciaran arrived at the site chosen for his monastery at Saigir, he is said to have found a wild boar already in residence.

> The boar fled from Ciaran at first, but afterwards came back gently to him; and this boar was Ciaran's first monk, and cut with his tusks the wattles for the church.
>
> Afterwards other monks came to Ciaran, to wit, a fox, a badger and a wolf, and were obedient to him.

Still more convenient for the requirements of the Patrick legend were the curious fragments which occur in the earliest sources for Ciaran and point to his association with a "voyage" tradition of mystic pilgrimage. Another note in the *Martyrology of Oengus* makes an intriguing reference to a "wonderful manuscript" set down within living memory of the saint and, evidently, still extant at Saigir at least as late as the eighth century:

> Now Cairnech the Bald was the scribe of Ciaran of Saigir. It is he who wrote the wonderful manuscript, namely "Ciaran's Journey," with its many various illustrations and this book still remains at Saigir. And let everyone who shall study it give a blessing on the soul of Cairnech the Bald, and on my own soul.

No other account of "Ciaran's Journey" has survived
but some knowledge of it would seem to have inspired
the Lismore *Litany of Pilgrim Saints* to invoke:

> The fifteen men who went with Ciaran of Sai-
> gir; *Per Iesum.*

The *Litany* refers to a long list of holy men, some of
whose "pilgrimages" are well known from other sources
while those of others are utterly obscure. The course
and destination of Ciaran's pilgrimage is unstated and
may not have been known to the Lismore author. It
was, after all, the act of pilgrimage as the pursuit of
the white martyrdom, rather than its destination which
merited a saint his inclusion in the *Litany,* but a
journey from Ireland to Rome would have been unimag-
inably hazardous in the fifth century and was not to
become a customary route of pilgrimage until later and
safer medieval centuries.

It would seem, then, to have been these references to
Ciaran's "voyage" tradition which inspired the later
invention of a pilgrimage to Rome as a device to enable
the meeting with Patrick, but the pilgrimage of the
historical Ciaran would have followed a very different
course. When the fragmentary evidence of the early
sources is brought together with that of the place-name
dedications, the course of "Ciaran's Journey" would
have brought him out of Ireland and into Scotland. Its
dates are, of course, unrecorded, but might be safely
placed around the time of the arrival of Fergus Mór
and the foundation of the kingdom of Scotic Dalriada,
which would account for Ciaran's activity in the
heartland of Fergus' territory around Campbeltown.

The monastery of Kilkerran was held in sufficiently
great esteem by the Cenél Gabrain to be chosen as the

burial-place of Aidan mac-Gabran, king of Alba, in 608 and was, in all probability, also the burial-place of his grandfather, Domangart, who is believed to have died in monastic retirement on Kintyre a hundred years earlier. The monastery may have begun with a founding community of "the fifteen men who went with Ciaran" invoked in the *Litany of Pilgrim Saints*. It may, otherwise, have grown up in association with the site of what had been Ciaran's hermit's cell and there is a fearsomely inaccessible cave hermitage, long called "St Ciaran's Cave," some five miles along the coast south-east of Campbeltown. On the floor of the cave has been found a sculptured stone incised with a symbol described as "the six-armed variety of the *Chi-Rho* monogram"[10] and surrounded by a border of square-key pattern. It may not be quite as old as Ciaran's time, indeed only very few carvings of Christian symbols are of fifth century provenance, but it is certainly very ancient and confirms the cave as a holy place of great antiquity.

Ciaran was buried in his monastery of Saigir and it is more than likely that he spent his later life there. If that had been the case, he could well have made his pilgrimage into Scotland earlier in his life, even some decades before Fergus founded the kingdom of Scotic Dalriada, and sought his white martyrdom amongst the earlier settlements of the Irish in Britain.

The roofless shell of a medieval chapel at Kilchiaran on the west side of the Rhinns of Islay stands today on what can be taken to be the site of Ciaran's cell. If the saint had crossed from Ireland before the royal house of Dalriada established itself on Kintyre, there is no reason why he should not have come first to Islay and into the territory of the Cenél nOengussa — a clan

whose name was already recorded in Ireland before
Fergus' time — before moving on from there, in the
way of the *peregrini,* to Kintyre.

Which enters, perhaps somewhat too far, into the
realm of speculation, but there is no doubt that the
wide mouth of Loch Indaal offered a safely sheltered
landfall to a curach crossing from Ireland and neither
is there any shortage of evidence for the significance of
"blue-green Ile" on the sea-road of the saints.

# ISLAY
# "Blue-green Ile"

The island of Islay is more often associated nowadays with single malt whisky than saints. To which I can only add a mention of the spurious, but still attractive, tradition that it was Patrick who first taught the art of distilling to the Irish and the more historical probability that it was the Irish Gael who first brought the *uisgue-beatha*, "water of life," to Islay.

The modern form of the island name of Islay is an anglicization of the same one which occurs in older Irish sources as *Ile* and in modern Gaelic as *Ìle*, but which makes its earliest appearance in Adamnan's seventh-century Latin as *Ilea insula* — a literal translation of the more ancient Irish Celtic name proposed by Professor W.J. Watson as meaning the "big-flanked island." Celtic names, for people as often as places, are most usually descriptive references to physical appearance, and Professor Watson adds the observation that "the peculiar shape of the island lends itself well to such an origin for its name."[11] So, indeed, it does and, like the Gaelic *ceann-tír* for the "headland" of Kintyre, the name reflects the prospect of Islay — with its twin promontories of the Rhinns and the Oa lying like great haunches on either side of the long sea-inlet of Loch Indaal — as it appears to an approach from Ireland.

Adamnan, in fact, uses the name *Ilea insula* only once in his *Life of Columba,* when he identifies the island as the home of a murderer whose own death was prophesied by Columba, but he makes another and more illuminating reference to Islay, even without specific use of the name, in his account of the miracle of St Cainnech's staff.

# The miracle of St Cainnech's crozier

Cainnech of Aghaboe, the son of a bard and an immediate contemporary of Columba, was born and raised in northern Derry. He studied for the church with Finnian at Clonard in Westmeath and with Mobi at Glasnevin near Dublin, at which time he formed his close friendship with Columba, who was also a student at one, if not both, of those monasteries. When the community at Glasnevin was broken up by the plague which struck Ireland in 544 and claimed the abbot Mobi among its victims, Columba made his way back to the north of Ireland and there founded his first monastery on the abandoned hillfort at Derry granted him by a royal kinsman. It would have been at much the same time that Cainnech went out of Ireland in search of a

hermitage, having first sought the advice of Finnian of
Clonard, according to a note in the *Martyrology of
Oengus.*

> When Cainnech went to visit Finnian, he asked
> him for a place of residence.
> "I see no place here now," said Finnian, "for
> others have taken up all the places before thee."
> "May there be a desert place there," said Cain-
> nech, "that is, in Alba."

There are Scottish place-name dedications to Cainnech to be found from Kintyre to the Great Glen —
some of them incorporating his English name-form of
"Kenneth" or its Scots variant of "Kenzie" — but J.F.
Kenney, the eminent authority on the early sources for
the Irish church, suspects that "it is probable that in
Scotland the majority of his churches were later
dedications." There is, nonetheless, sufficiently abun-
dant evidence in the early sources to convince Kenney
that Cainnech "spent some part of his early life in the
western isles of Scotland."[12] One of those Hebridean
hermitages must have been the otherwise unidentified
"Bird Island" where the early morning uproar so
greatly disrupted the first offices of the monastic day
that the saint had to command his seabird neighbours
to be silent, at least, until after Matins. The *Life of
Cainnech* — which survives in three medieval Latin
versions deriving from the same earlier Irish original
— tells how reluctantly he abandoned the life of a
hermit in the western sea to become a founder of
monasteries in Ireland.

> The saints of Ireland sent messages to Cainnech,
> having learned that he was living as a hermit in

Britain; and Cainnech was then brought back
from his hermitage against his will.

One personal characteristic is so consistently ascribed
to him by the early sources as to be taken as a genuine
eccentricity of the historical Cainnech. He was, as
Adamnan's account of the miraculous recovery of his
abbot's staff confirms, notoriously absent-minded.

> Cainnech embarked for Ireland from the harbour
> of Iona, and forgot to take his staff with him.
> After his departure, the staff was found on the
> shore and given into the hands of Columba, who,
> on his return home, brought it into the oratory,
> and remained there for a very long time alone in
> prayer. Cainnech, meanwhile, on approaching
> the island of Oidech, suddenly felt pricked at
> heart at the thought of his forgetfulness, and
> was deeply afflicted by it. But after some time,
> leaving the vessel and falling upon his knees in
> prayer on the ground, he found before him on
> the turf of the little land of Aitech the staff
> which, in his forgetfulness, he had left behind
> him at the landing place on Iona. He was greatly
> surprised at its being thus brought to him by
> divine power, and gave thanks to God.

Adamnan's account hinges on the great importance
attached by the ancient Irish church to a holy man's
crook-headed wooden staff or *bachall,* closely associated
with the miraculous and revered as the principal
personal relic of a saint, but it is another aspect of his
story which is of more especial significance here.

Adamnan describes Cainnech's approaching *insula
Oidecha,* "the island of Oidech," and his Oidech corre-

sponds to the name *Odeich* used in another source of seventh-century origin to identify the round-ended peninsula which forms the eastern flank of Loch Indaal and is known now as the Oa. Adamnan's "island of" the Oa can be thus firmly identified, from his "little land of Aitech," as the islet marked on modern maps as Texa.

The mutation of *Aitech* into Texa is a consequence of the ninth-century Norse settlement of the Hebrides which followed in the wake of the first viking raids. The "Ai-" prefix had probably already been dropped from the island name even before it was re-cast in the Norse form of *Techs ey* ('tech island), which was to appear already spelled as *Texa* in the list of islands set down by John of Fordun in his fourteenth-century *Chronicle of the Scottish Nation.*

Helant (Isle of) Texa, with a monastic cell.

Fordun's "monastic cell" was the same medieval chapel, of which the ruins are still to be seen on Texa, accorded considerable prestige under the medieval Lordship of the Isles and generously endowed with some fine sculptured crosses, one of the finest of them a gift of Reginald, progenitor of Clan Ranald and son of John of Islay, the first Lord of the Isles, in the second half of the fourteenth century.

Whether the medieval chapel stood over the site of a more ancient monastic cell is nowhere recorded, but Texa does lie just a little way offshore from the promontory of Dunyvaig, a place-name which would seem to have defeated every attempt to trace its origin. It has been proposed as deriving in some wise from the Gaelic *naomh,* "holy" or "holy man," perhaps *Dún Naomháig,* "fort of the little saint" or even "fort of the holy harbour," although the local pronunciation in use since

medieval times would not properly correspond. The
crumbling shell of the fortress on Dunyvaig is a survival from the medieval Lordship of the Isles, but one
which may well have been built on a still earlier
defensive site, perhaps even that of the capital fortress
of the Cenél nOengussa. The enigma remains, but the
possibility of a monastic cell on an island lying just
offshore from a promontory fort at the time of Cainnech's arrival from Iona in the second half of the sixth
century can still not be entirely discounted.

By contrast with the uncertainties surrounding Texa
and Dunyvaig, the sea-route which brought Cainnech
to Islay *en voyage* from Iona to Ireland can be deduced
with some precision from Adamnan's evidence. A south-
easterly course from Iona, passing in the lee of Colonsay but safely to the west of the hazardous Strait of
Corryvreckan between Jura and Scarba, would have
carried his curach into and through the Sound of Islay
to round the south-east corner of the island. At which
point the saint would have seen the cliffs of the Oa
peninsula, wild and peat-clad realm of chough and
raven, come into view in the further distance and
directly ahead of him the isle of Texa, "the little land of
Aitech" where the *bachall* he had left behind on Iona
lay awaiting his arrival. Given reasonable visibility, he
would have been able to make out Rathlin Island on
the horizon and behind it the northern coast of Ireland
some twenty miles away to the south.

Cainnech would seem to have been a frequent visitor to
Iona and there were, at one time, two ancient dedications to him on the island — a *Cill Chainnich* and
*Cladh Cainnech,* "Cainnech's Cemetery" — so there is
every reason to take Adamnan's indication of his sea-
route as the one customarily followed by the curach

traffic between Iona and Ireland. His *Life of Columba* contains a number of references to monastic visitors from Ireland on Iona in Columba's own time and the Irish annals enter regular voyaging to and from Ireland by successive abbots of Iona throughout the seventh and eighth centuries.

Nowhere in these early sources, however, is there any reliable indication of the duration of the voyage but that information can be sought now in the writings of a more recent seafarer. In 1976 the historian Tim Severin set out from the coast of Kerry in an authentic reconstruction of a sixth-century curach to retrace the supposedly legendary sea-road of St Brendan the Voyager. Dr Severin's course led him up the west coast of Ireland, through the Hebridean archipelago, and then, by way of the Faroe Islands, to Iceland and, ultimately, the coast of Labrador, but the passage of immediate interest here is his crossing from Bally-hoorisky on the north-west corner of Donegal to Iona.

While Severin did not follow precisely the same course indicated for Cainnech — sailing, obviously, in the opposite direction, and bearing to the west, rather than the east, of Islay and of Colonsay — his *Curragh Brendan* completed the crossing within two days. There are so many variables involved — wind and weather, to name but two — as to make precise comparison impossible, but when Severin was able to put out from Ballyhoorisky in the afternoon and make landfall on Iona on the second morning following, it would be perfectly reasonable to assume an approximate forty-eight hour duration for monastic seafarers undertaking the same voyage in closely similar craft some fourteen centuries earlier.

Two days' sailing, then, between Iona and Ireland would place Islay at the most convenient point to make

an overnight stop and such would have been the most
plausible reason for Cainnech's curach putting in to
Texa, where even a modest monastic settlement would
have been able to provide hospitality for a distinguished Irish abbot and his companions on passage
home from Iona.

It has even been suggested to me that the "cell"
component in place-names found throughout the
Hebrides can be taken as the monastic equivalent of
the "Bed & Breakfast" signs so widely in evidence —
and in many of the same places — today and, for all its
jocularity, there is a good measure of truth in that
suggestion. It would be quite reasonable, then, to
propose Islay as the customary overnight port-of-call
for voyages between Ireland and Iona and thus explain
the prominence of Columban associations among the
place-name dedications to be found on the island. All
the parishes on Islay today include one name with the
dedicatory "Kil-" prefix and, of those five place-name
dedications, no less than three might be shown to
commemorate saints closely connected with the Columban church.

The earlier of the two parish names with no Iona
connection is Kilchiaran at the top of the Rhinns
peninsula on the west coast of Islay, which can be
grouped with similar place-names on Kintyre as
indicating the presence of the fifth-century Ciaran of
Saigir. The other — Kilarrow, a corruption of the older
"Kilmolrow" from the Gaelic *Cille Mhaoil Rubha,*
"Maelrubha's Cell" — is some two hundred years
younger and can be dated, with unusual precision on
the evidence of the Irish annals, to the year 671 when
"Maelrubha sailed to Britain."

# Kilarrow and Maelrubha

Maelrubha of Applecross is more widely honoured by place-name dedications in Scotland than any saint other than Columba and, like Columba, he came of a noble Irish line of the northern Uí Neill.

Eighth in direct descent from Niall of the Nine Hostages, Maelrubha was born in the south-east of Derry in 642. His father was of the Cenél Eoghain (the clan of Eoghan, son of Niall) of Tyrone and Inish-owen, but it was the kindred of his mother, a niece of St Comgall of Bangor, which was to bear the greatest influence on his destiny. By reason of his blood-kinship to its founding abbot, Maelrubha entered on his monastic career at Bennchor, now Bangor in Down, one of the most important monasteries in seventh-century Ireland and certainly one of the largest. The *Litany of Irish Saints* tells of "the four thousand monks under the Rule of Comgall at Bennchor" and Maelrubha might well have become their abbot, the *comarba* of Comgall, had he not chosen the way of the white martyrdom.

There is no surviving *Life* of Maelrubha and all that is known of him must be gleaned from a few summary entries in the Irish annals, genealogies, and calendars of saints, to supplement the quatrain in celebration of his feast-day entered in the *Martyrology of Oengus* under April 21st.

> In Alba in purity,
> After abandoning all happiness,
> Hath gone from us to his mother,
> Our brother Maelrubha.

There is one other very valuable source for Maelrubha in the evidence of place-name dedications from
which it has been possible to trace the course of his
pilgrimage into Alba and Kilarrow, "Maelrubha's cell"
on Islay, has the strongest claim to have been the
saint's first foundation in Scotland. If he had sailed
over from his own clan country of Derry, the wide sea
inlet of Loch Indaal would have offered the best sheltered course of approach for his curach, so it would
seem to be no mere coincidence that Kilarrow is located
at the head of Loch Indaal.

From Islay, the Maelrubha dedications mark out the
northward course of his two-year journey along the
west coast of the mainland, by way of Kintyre, Oban,
and Arisaig, to Applecross, *Apur Crossan* or "the mouth
of the Crossan," and it was there in 673, according to
the Irish annals, that "Maelrubha founded his church."
The Crossan was the old name for the stream — called
locally in the Gaelic *Amhain Maree,* "Maelrubha's
river" — flowing beside the place the saint chose for his
monastery on a bay looking out across the Inner Sound
to the island of Raasay and beyond it the great peaks
of Skye.

Thomas Pennant's account of his travels in Scotland
in 1769 mentions Maelrubha as being "regarded as the
patron of all the coast between Applecross and Loch
Brain" (by which he meant Loch Broom in Wester Ross)
and the concentration of place-name evidence confirms
that region, especially if it included Skye, to have been
the saint's central area of activity. The precise political
geography of seventh-century Scotland is always
blurred, but Applecross itself must have lain on, if not
beyond, the frontier of Dalriadic territory, and there is
ample evidence to show Maelrubha's monks, if not the
saint himself, journeying out to the islands, even as far

as Harris, and east through the mountain passes into territories which can be considered then to have been "Pictland." All of which must be set, as was the white martyrdom of Columba a century before, into the political context of the 670s.

In the absence of any *Life* of Maelrubha, there is no explanation of what might have prompted the saint to journey as far to the north as he did, but the combined evidence of annal entries and place-names indicates his crossing from Ireland to Islay in 671. His time on Kintyre and elsewhere in Argyll must be placed, then, between 671 and the foundation of Applecross in 673, which was also the period of Bruide mac-Beli's succession, around 672, as high-king of Picts. The gradual process of the establishment of Christianity in Pictland was by then well advanced and Bruide himself, the son of the king of the Britons of Strathclyde, was assuredly Christian. He was held in high regard, even as a personal friend, by Adamnan, who became abbot of Iona in 679 and officiated at Bruide's burial there in 693. Bruide's reign marked a dramatic upturn in the political fortunes of the Picts which reached its high point in 685 when he inflicted a crushing defeat on Northumbria at the battle of Nechtansmere and threw the imperium of the northern English back south of the Forth. The coincidence of an Irish holy man already established in Dalriada travelling so far north to found his monastery within a year of the succession of so powerful a high-king of Picts on such excellent terms with the Irish church in Scotland cannot, I would suggest, be entirely accidental.

To which suggestion might be added just one curious footnote in the form of a fragment of bardic praise poetry offering up gratitude to Christ for Bruide's victory at Nechtansmere. These verses are preserved in

just one set of Irish annals where they are attributed
by the annalist to Riagal of Bangor, an Irish monk
apparently attached to the Pictish court at the time of
the battle and probably himself an eye-witness of the
conflict, who would have most plausibly come into
Pictland by way of the foundation of his fellow monk of
Bangor at Apur Crossan. The evidence of Riagal can be
taken to confirm Maelrubha being joined by monks
from Bangor who followed him in their own quest for
the white martyrdom of exile. He would have brought
with him from Ireland a number of companions to form
the core of his monastic community, first on Islay and
eventually at Applecross, and attracted more recruits
to his *familia* at each stage of his travels.

Applecross, which represented a monastic estate
extending over some six square miles, evidently grew
into a very large monastery indeed and yet it was still
a daughter house of Bangor which maintained a close
relationship with the great monastery in Down even
after Maelrubha's death in 722. In the way of all the
monasteries of the Hebrides, Applecross maintained
contact with many of its own outlying cells and, of
necessity, with its associated monasteries in Ireland by
means of the sea-traffic so customary as to command
an entry in the annals only in the event of a major
disaster. One such was the death by drowning of the
*comarba* of Maelrubha on voyage between Applecross
and Ireland entered in the *Annals of Tigernach* at 737.

> Failbe, son of Guaire, successor of Maelrubha of
> Applecross, was drowned in the deep sea with
> his sailors, twenty-two in number.

All of which must seem some distance removed from
*Ilea insula,* although the annalist's reference to "the

deep sea" might be taken to indicate the waters where Failbe perished as those of the North Channel separating Ireland from Islay and Kintyre and Adamnan tells of Columba's foreknowledge concerning a prominent Irish cleric in peril at sea on just that crossing. "Colman, son of Beogna" is entered in the calendars as Colman of Lynally in Offaly, but the "Brecan's whirlpool" meant by Adamnan's *Coire Brecain* is the one now known as Sloc na Mara off the coast of Antrim and not the Sound of Corryvreckan between Scarba and Jura, which does not appear under that name until the fourteenth century.

> "Colman, the son of Beogna, has just now set out on a voyage to us, and is in great danger in the rolling tides of Brecan's whirlpool. He is sitting at the prow and raising both his hands to heaven. He is also blessing that angry and dreadful sea, yet in this the Lord only frightens him, for the ship in which he is shall not be wrecked in the storm, but this is rather to excite him to pray more fervently, that by God's favour he may escape the danger of his voyage, and reach us in safety."

# Kilmeny and Eithne

Adamnan makes so many references to voyages between Ireland and Iona that it is hardly surprising to find so many individuals who feature in his *Life of Columba* named also in dedications found on Islay, the island serving as the customary port of call on that crossing. Foremost among those place-name dedications are the three parish names, each of them representing a monastic settlement in Adamnan's time, which might be shown to have Columban associations.

Kilmeny in the north east of Islay is taken by every authority to be a corruption of *Cill M'Eithne,* "Cell of My Eithne," the "M'-" prefix representing a term of endearment and signifying a dedication in honour of a saint who may not necessarily have been at that place. *Cill M'Eithne,* then, would indicate a monastery dedicated in affectionate memory of a St Eithne and there is just one probable candidate of that name, the Eithne named by Adamnan as the mother of Columba.

Whether Eithne ever came out of Ireland is unrecorded, but there is a stone on one of the Garvellach islands to the north of Jura which is claimed by tradition to mark her grave. Whether in fact it does so is as immaterial as it is unlikely, but it must nonetheless represent a lost tradition of Eithne following her son into the western sea and one which might well have also associated her in some way with Islay. What can be said of Eithne is that her cult was still highly regarded in the later seventh century, when Adamnan wrote his *Life of Columba,* on the evidence of its third and most mystic book — "Of the Visions of Angels" — opening with a chapter describing Eithne's prophetic vision of her son's destiny.

> On a certain night between the conception and birth of the venerable man, an angel of the Lord appeared to his mother in dreams, bringing to her, as he stood by her, a certain robe of extraordinary beauty, in which the most beautiful colours, as it were, of all the flowers seemed to be portrayed. After a short time he asked it back, and took it out of her hands, and having raised it and spread it out, he let it fly through the air.

But she, being sad at the loss of it, said to the
man of venerable aspect, "Why dost thou take
this lovely cloak away from me so soon?"...

"Because this mantle is so exceedingly honourable that thou cannot longer retain it with thee."
When this was said, the woman saw the robe
gradually receding from her in its flight; and
then it expanded until its width exceeded the
plains, and in all its measurements was larger
than the mountains and forests. Then she heard
the following words: "Woman, do not grieve, for
to the man to whom thou has been joined by the
marriage bond, thou shalt bring forth a son of so
beautiful a character that he shall be reckoned
among his own people as one of the prophets of
God, and hath been predestined by God to be the
leader of innumerable souls to the heavenly
country." At these words the woman awoke from
her sleep.

The same vision is included in the Irish *Life of
Columcille,* set down in Derry some five hundred years
after Adamnan, but in a still more elaborate rendering
which has the robe being seen to spread across land
and sea from the shores of Mayo to the Moray Firth.

Eithne herself interpreted that vision and said
then: "I will bear a son," said she, "and his
teaching shall extend throughout the lands of
Erin and Alba."

Whether Adamnan was drawing on an Irish tradition,
whether the Derry hagiographer was elaborating on
Adamnan, or whether both versions draw on some still
more ancient common original long since lost is un-

known. What can be said is that the cult of Eithne as
the saintly mother of the great saint of the Gael is
known to have flourished as early as the seventh
century and as late as the twelfth, so it would be safe
to date the foundation of Cill M'Eithne on Islay within
that period, and probably very much closer to the time
of Adamnan than to that of the Derry hagiographer.

# Kilchoman and Comman

The foundation of Kilchoman, or *Cille Chomain,* can be
firmly dated to the seventh century. There are a
number of Commans in the Irish calendars of saints,
but the one commemorated on Islay died in 688 and his
feast-day is entered under March 18th. To his entry in
the *Kalendar of Scottish Saints* is added the note that
"his church is Kilchoman in the Rhinns of Islay." The
same Comman is to be also identified with the "respected priest" named by Adamnan as his source for an
account of "the angelic splendour of the light which
Virgnous...saw coming down on St Columba in the
church, on a winter's night, when the brethren were at
rest."

*Virgnous* is Adamnan's Latin name-form for Fergna,
the third *comarba* of Columba and abbot of Iona from
605 until 623. One winter's night when Fergna was
still a young monk on Iona he had "entered the church
alone to pray, while the others were asleep and he
prayed fervently in a little side-chamber attached to
the walls of the oratory."

> After a considerable interval...the venerable
> Columba entered the same sacred house, and
> along with him, at the same time, a golden light

that came down from the highest heavens and
filled that part of the church. Even the separate
recess of the side-chamber, where Virgnous was
striving to hide himself as much as he could,
was also filled, to his great alarm, with some of
the brilliance of that heavenly light.... And as no
one can look directly at the summer sun in his
mid-day splendour, so Virgnous could not at all
bear this heavenly brightness...so much terrified
by the splendour, almost as dreadful as lightning, that no strength remained in him.

Visitations of heavenly light feature so prominently in
the Adamnan *Life* as to form the great theme of its
concluding book and it is a phenomenon which will call
for further consideration here, but the immediate
significance of Fergna's unearthly experience is the
channel by which Adamnan learned of it.

Comman, a respected priest and sister's son to
Virgnous, solemnly assured me, Adamnan, of the
truth of the vision I have just described, and he
added, moreover, that he heard the story from
the lips of the abbot Virgnous, his own uncle,
who, as far as he could, had seen that vision.

Comman's entry in the *Martyrology of Donegal* includes
an illuminating note of his lineage in Columba's own
clan of the Cenél Conaill as the "son of Ernan, of the
race of Conall Gulban, son of Niall," which reveals him
to have been the nephew of not one but two abbots of
Iona — Fergna and his successor Segine — and also
the brother of a third.

Comman's brother, Cummene the White, succeeded
as the *comarba* of Columba in 657 and held the abbacy

for some twelve years. He died in 669 and his entry in the *Martyrology of Donegal* adds a note to his genealogy confirming that "he wrote the *Life of Columcille* in 134 chapters." Cummene's *Life* of Iona's founding saint, the earliest one on record, has been long since lost, but was well-known to Adamnan as one of his "written authorities anterior to my own times" on which he drew for his own *Life of Columba*. He did, in fact, include in his *Life* an important passage which he acknowledges as being extracted from Cummene's book.

The common ground between these two Iona *Lives* of its founding saint extends also to the circumstances in which each came to be written, because both were set down in response to a perceived crisis in the prestige and authority of Iona as the mother church of the Columban *paruchia*. That crisis which beset Iona throughout the seventh and into the eighth century grew out of what has since been called the "Paschal Controversy," the dispute as to the proper calculation of the date in each year on which the church should celebrate Easter. As the celebration of the Resurrection of Christ which stood at the very centre of the Christian faith, Easter was the most important festival in the church calendar and it was, thus, considered essential that it should be celebrated at the same time throughout the Christian world.

In consequence of the isolation of Celtic Ireland from the continent through much of the fifth and sixth centuries, a series of revisions to the system of calculating the date of Easter were authorised by the Pope in Rome for adoption throughout the universal church without being communicated to the Irish church. The mission of Augustine to England in 597 established the Roman orthodoxy in the southern Anglo-Saxon kingdoms from the point of their first conversion. The churches of southern Ireland, coming once again into contact with the continent at much the same time, initially resisted the Roman orthodoxy but eventually aquiesced following a visit of Irish envoys to Rome in 632. Dispute over the question had already arisen within the Columban church by the following year, when the abbot of Durrow, the most southerly of the Columban foundations in Ireland, defended his own adoption of the Roman Easter in a sharply ironic letter to Segine, abbot of Iona.

> Rome is in error, Jerusalem in error, Alexandria
> in error, the whole world is in error; only the
> Scots and the Britons know what is correct...

Segine's reponse has not survived, but was not likely to have been sympathetic. Iona's authority was not to be challenged and the "Celtic" dating of Easter had been recognized by its own founding saint Columba on the authority of St John the Evangelist, whose Gospel had always been held in the greatest esteem by the ancient Irish church.

Within just a few years of the letter from Durrow, Segine further advanced the prestige of his church by the foundation of a daughter house on the island of Lindisfarne in Northumbria at the invitation of Oswald, king of the northern English and effective overlord of Anglo-Saxon England. For nearly thirty years, the Columban foundation on Lindisfarne, the "Iona in the east," provided the great wellspring for the conversion of pagan English kingdoms to Christianity until 664, when Oswy, Oswald's brother and successor as king of Northumbria, summoned the Synod of Whitby. There he decided in favour of the Roman dating of Easter and against the Celtic orthodoxy in his

kingdom, the Irish bishop of Lindisfarne returned to
Iona, and the royal church of the most powerful kingdom of England was lost to the Columban *paruchia.*

If the first intention of the hagiographer was the
presentation of his saint as an exemplar of sanctity, it
would seem that his further purpose was the defence of
his principal church, and it was very soon after the
Synod of Whitby that Cummene the White, abbot of
Iona, set down his *Life of Columcille.* His sources were
the recollections of Columba gathered by his uncle, the
abbot Segine, from aged monks on Iona and his intention was the restoration of the authority of both his
monastery and its founding saint, but the Paschal
controversy was to long outlive Cummene. What had
begun as a dispute prompted by ecclesiastical failure of
communication became a whirlpool of acrimony sucking
into itself a host of more worldly imperatives of prestige, power, land, and tribal rivalry.

When Adamnan, the ninth abbot of Iona, visited
Northumbria on a diplomatic mission at the behest of
the high-king of Ireland in 686 and again in 688 to
renew his friendship with learned Northumbrian
churchmen, he came to accept the Roman orthodoxy.
On his return to Iona he sought to persuade his community to join him in that acceptance, fearing that self-
imposed exclusion from the catholic unity could only
further damage the standing of Iona, as he had seen it
to have done in Northumbria. He was no less anxious
to preserve the reputation of his saint from the disre-
gard in which the world appeared now to hold his
principal church, and to that end began work on his
*Life of Columba.* In so doing, he succeeded in setting
down the most important work of record to have
survived from the ancient Irish church, but failed,
nonetheless, to persuade his own community to follow

him into the fold of catholic unity. It was not until twelve years after Adamnan's death that Egbert, a monk of Lindisfarne who had attached himself to Iona, finally achieved its formal acceptance of the Roman orthodoxy in 716, but even then it would seem that a dissident element in the community held out for almost half a century. The details of schism on Iona in the eighth-century monastery are far from clear, but there would seem to have been long periods when there were two abbots, apparently representing rival tribal loyalties, on the island and there can be little doubt of the decline in Iona's prestige through the seven decades between the death of Adamnan in 704 and the succession of Bresal to the abbacy in 772.

Bresal's origins and lineage are obscure, but his thirty years as its abbot marked the restoration of the stature of Iona to its last great peak before the onslaught of the vikings. It was the time when a high-king of Ireland chose the island monastery for his retirement and his final resting-place and an Iona craftsman carved the magnificent high cross still to be seen today at Kildalton on Islay.

## The enigma of Kildalton

Standing a full nine feet tall and carved from a single block of local bluestone, the eighth-century cross beside the medieval chapel at Kildalton on the south-east side of Islay is the only free-standing Celtic ring cross to have survived entirely intact in Scotland. The two other examples of crosses of the same style and period carved by craftsmen of what is called the "Iona school" are still preserved on Iona, but both are incomplete.

The one known as the "St Martin" cross is lacking both
its arms and the other, called the "St John" cross, is
preserved only in a reconstruction from fragments of
the original, which is known to have been shattered on
more than one occasion.

The Kildalton Cross is not only unique of its kind,
but a masterpiece of its age, the counterpart in carved
stone of the Book of Kells on vellum. Its cultural
significance was best described in the last century by
one of the great authorities on early Christian art in
Scotland, Joseph Anderson.

> The special feature of its character is the intense
> Celticism of its art. No other cross now standing
> exhibits this in such a striking manner. Its two
> panels, filled with divergent spirals and trumpet
> patterns, and mingled with circles enclosing
> groups of spirals, wherever they might be found
> and in whatever material they might be exe-
> cuted, would be certainly recognized as products
> of Celtic art. Nothing like them can be instanced
> among the art-products of any other people or
> any other time.[13]

All of which leads up to the great question which
hangs over the Kildalton Cross: why was this place
chosen some twelve hundred years ago to be endowed
with so outstanding a masterwork of monastic sculp-
ture? There does seem to be the quality of a holy place
about the walled kirkyard under a bracken slope at
Kildalton which transcends the gaunt warrior on
the medieval tombstone, the roofless shell of the
thirteenth-century chapel, and even the aura of the
weathered grey-blue stone of the cross itself. All that
remains of the monastery which was in that place

before the cross was raised is the dedication encoded in the name Kildalton, but there is no likely saint *Daltán* entered anywhere in the Irish calendars, so it would seem not to have been a personal name. It might, perhaps, represent some form of cognomen and there the translation of the Gaelic name-form provides a clue: *Cill Daltan,* "Church of the Fosterling."

The reference to a "Rectory of St John at Kildalton" in a document of 1548 has prompted the suggestion that the "Church of the Fosterling" represents a coded dedication to St John the Evangelist who is sometimes called the "foster-son of Christ," but it has won little support. The monastery at Kildalton was in existence by the end of the eighth century and probably founded still earlier, when dedications in the Celtic west did not invoke the patronage of scriptural saints, but instead commemorated the name of the founding holy man or his patron. The identification of the holy man commemorated at Kildalton must be restricted, at best, to the realm of probability rather than that of certainty, but there is one saint eminently well-qualified with probabilities and who has, thus far, been apparently overlooked.

The presence of such an outstanding "Iona school" cross at Kildalton and the predominance of Columban dedications on Islay — no less than five to Columcille despite there being no mention in any early source of his ever visiting the island — would direct the search for "The Fosterling" into the orbit of Iona. There is in the *Life of Baithene,* Columba's first cousin and closest disciple, a passage which may well hold the key to the origin of the Kildalton dedication.

The testimony of St Columba himself concerning him.

For he said that his pupil Baithene, and John
the Evangelist, Christ's pupil, were not dissimi-
lar in purest innocence, and in wisest simplicity,
and in the discipline of the severity of their per-
fect works; that nevertheless their teachers were
widely different in their customs.

The tradition of the "fosterling" in Celtic Ireland very
probably originated as the schooling of the warrior
before being adopted by the church and was certainly
well-established as the custom of monastic training in
the sixth century. Columba himself began his education
as the fosterling of Cruithnecan, who is described by
Adamnan as "a priest of blameless life into whose care
the blessed youth was confided," and Columba similarly
undertook the education of his cousin Baithene, some
fifteen years his junior.

Like so many other *Lives* of Irish saints, the *Life of
Baithene* is known only from a medieval Latin version
deriving from an original set down even as early as the
first quarter of the seventh century and very probably
on Iona, but containing very much less historical
substance than is to be found in the many references to
Baithene in the Adamnan *Life of Columba.*

The seventh-century list of the twelve men who
accompanied Columba on his pilgrimage to Britain
begins with "Baithene, who is also called Conin," so
*Baithene* — Adamnan's Latin form of the Irish *Baithín*
— would seem, like *Columcille,* to have been a monastic name. The dates of the historical Baithene are the
subject of some confusion in the early sources, but the
*Annals of Tigernach* enter his birth at 536. He would
certainly have been only in his later twenties at the
time of his accompanying Columba to Scotland in 563,
but had already been the abbot of a Columban founda-

tion near Raphoe in Donegal. The evidence of Adamnan
— indicating him to have been placed in charge of
penitents on the island of Hinba and prior of another
Columban foundation on Tiree — confirms that he was
an able monastic administrator as well as an accomplished scribe and arable farmer.

Blood-kin and spiritual intimate of its founding
saint, Baithene was the natural successor to the abbacy
of Iona and Adamnan's account of Columba's last day
on earth tells of the aged saint transcribing a psalter
as he approached the hour of his death.

> "Here," said he, "at the end of the page, I must
> stop; and what follows let Baithene write."

Baithene was over sixty in 597 and his tenure as abbot
of Iona was destined to be of no great duration. Most
sources record his abbacy as lasting three years,
although one indicates his outliving Columba by just
twelve months. All are agreed, however, that both
saints died on June 9th and the *Martyrology of Oengus*
enters the two names together under that date.

> Baithín, high, angelical,
> Columcille the lustrous,
> always thou should put their feast
> on the same day of their solar month.

The evidence of Oengus is especially important here
because it was set down at much the same time as the
Kildalton Cross was raised and confirms the cult of
Baithene the Fosterling to have been held in high
honour two full centuries after his death in 600.

That high honour is further confirmed in the note to
the *Martyrology of Oengus* preserving the curious

exchange between Columcille and Baithín concerning
a vision of heavenly thrones.

> 'Tis then Baithín related to him a noteworthy
> vision, to wit, three thrones were seen by him in
> heaven, namely a throne of gold, and a throne of
> silver, and a throne of glass.
>
> "That is clear," says Columcille, "Ciaran [of
> Clonmacnois], son of the wright has the throne
> of gold on account of his honour and because of
> his hospitality.
>
> "Thou thyself, O Baithín, has the throne of
> silver because of the purity and lustre of thy
> devotion.
>
> "The throne of glass is mine, for though my
> devotion is fair, I am often frail and carnal."

It must be said that there is nowhere any record of
Baithene founding his own church on Islay or presiding
over any daughter house of Iona there, but neither does
the "Church of the Fosterling" resemble a dedication to
a founding saint. Its form would suggest instead the
commemoration of an event in the life of a saint which
was associated in some way with that place — an
association long since lost, but once held in such great
esteem as to command so impressive a monument as
the Kildalton Cross — and the probable identity of that
saint must be Baithene, "high, angelical," fosterling of
Columcille.

# "The island of St Finlaggan"

By contrast with the enigma of Kildalton, the island called Eilean Mor in Loch Finlaggan holds pride of place in the historical record of Islay, because there, until just five hundred years ago, stood the last royal capital of Celtic Scotland. The gaunt fangs of ruined wall and gable on an isle in the loch are all that remains now of the seat of the Lordship of the Isles. There also stood a chapel built over the site of the more ancient cell of a holy man commemorated in Eilean Mor's still more ancient name of the "Island of St Finlaggan."

Finlaggan is a later corruption of Findlugan, "disciple and brother of St Fintan of Dunblesque" according to a note in the *Martyrology of Oengus*. The *Life of Fintan* tells how Findlugan lived as a monk in his brother's monastery at Dunblesque (now Doon in Limerick) until he "crossed into Alba...where he remained until his death."

Adamnan contributes rather more detail to what is known of the white martyrdom of Findlugan and identifies him as the holy man to whose courage Columba owed his life.

> On one occasion when the blessed man [Columba] was living in the island of Hinba, and set about excommunicating some destroyers of churches...one of their wicked associates was instigated by the devil to rush on the saint with a spear, on purpose to kill him. To prevent this, one of the brethren, named Findlugan, put on the saint's cowl (an abbot's cowl being of white wool to distinguish it from the undyed wool of

those worn by his monks) and interposed himself, being ready to die for the holy man. But in
a wonderful way the saint's garment served as a
kind of strong and impenetrable fence which
could not be pierced by the thrust of a very
sharp spear though made by a powerful man,
but remained untouched, and he who had it on
was safe and uninjured under the protection of
such a guard.

The eastward prospect from Loch Finlaggan, towards
the great slopes of the Paps of Jura across the Sound
of Islay, is one of strikingly characteristic Hebridean
grandeur.

When Findlugan, in the later years of his white
martyrdom of exile, looked out from his island hermitage he must have surely more than once remembered
the day when he won his own very honourable mention
in Adamnan's book, because the name by which he
would have called the land he saw across the Sound
was the island of Hinba.

# JURA
# "The Island of Hinba"

Around the time of the death of Aristotle and some three hundred years before Christ, the Greek seafarer Pytheas is said to have circumnavigated the British Isles.

His account of that voyage has been long since lost, but not before substantial extracts from it had found their way into the works of many classical geographers. Both Pliny in the first century AD and Ptolemy a hundred years after him were able to draw on the evidence of Pytheas and, in so doing, to preserve the most ancient record of the island names of the western sea.

It was not until a full thousand years after Pytheas that Adamnan was to set down a comparable record of

Hebridean island names in his *Life of Columba* of the
late seventh century AD, when the earlier Celtic and
pre-Celtic name-forms had been transformed by the
Goidelic Celtic language which accompanied the Irish
settlement of the west of Scotland. It is, nonetheless,
remarkable just how many of the island names in
modern usage can be recognized as obvious descendants of those mentioned by Adamnan and before him
by Ptolemy and Pliny quoting from Pytheas of the third
century BC.

The Isle of Mull, for example, is the anglicized form
of the Gaelic *Eilean Muileach* which is as clearly
recognizable in Ptolemy's *Malaios* (from Pytheas) as it
is in Adamnan's *Malea insula*. So too is Pytheas' *Skitis*
to be recognized in Adamnan's *Scia insula* and the
modern Isle of Skye, but there are other names found
in Adamnan which have been totally obscured by the
impact of the Norse settlement of the Hebrides from
the end of the eighth century. The legacy of the seafaring northmen is naturally most prominent on the
modern map of Scotland amongst those place-names
with maritime associations and coastal locations. Thus
Tarbert — a name which occurs with confusing frequency from Harris down to Kintyre — originated as
the Norse *tairm-bert,* "an overbringing," signifying a
neck of land sufficiently narrow to allow a longship to
be carried across it. The Norse elements in mountain
names throughout the Western Isles indicate their
navigational importance to the longship steersman and
it was, of course, inevitable that viking landseekers
should have soon given their own names to their island
landfalls. Adamnan's *Elen,* for example, has never been
firmly identified. While it might just possibly have been
Nave Island off the north of Islay, all that can be said
with certainty is that *Elen* can have no connection with

the modern Gaelic *eilean,* which is a loan-word of pure
Scandinavian descent from the Norse *eyland,* or
"island."

# The quest for "Hinba"

Neither is there any modern island name to be recognized as the obvious descendant of Adamnan's *Hinba
insula,* "the island of Hinba." This "island of Hinba" is
presented by Adamnan as a place of great significance
for his saint and, in consequence, its identification
commands a strategic importance for what is known of
the historical Columba. While he offers the very least
indication of the island's whereabouts, Adamnan does
confirm a short list of significant facts about "Hinba."

It was the site, first of all, of a monastery founded
not long after Columba's arrival in Scotland and,
almost certainly, before that on Iona. It was also the
island chosen for another, and apparently separate,
community of voluntary anchorites. The monastery was
used to accommodate a number of *penitens* or penitents, monastic recruits who had trangressed at some
point in their training and been placed under a more
stringent regime in the hope of rehabilitating them for
admission to the *familia.* Both of the men named by
Adamnan as priors on Hinba, Ernan and Baithene,
were close kin to Columba who himself is described, on
different occasions, as both "living on" and "visiting"
the island and there experiencing two of his most
impressive spiritual visitations.

The only fragmentary indications of the location of
Hinba to be inferred from the *Life of Columba* are its
reasonable proximity to Iona and its situation on the
sea-route from Ireland, both of which could apply to

any number of islands and both of which might be satisfied by the group lying to the south-east of Mull and known as the Garvellachs. Impressive examples of drystone-built "beehive" cells, or *clocháin,* are still to be seen on the most southerly of the Garvellachs — known as Elachnave, from the Gaelic *Eileach nan naomh,* "the holy rock" — and it would seem to have been these which led nineteenth-century scholars to pronounce this rocky islet as Adamnan's "Hinba." Their proposal was widely accepted until the publication in 1926 of W.J. Watson's work on Scotland's Celtic place-names which demonstrated beyond doubt that Elachnave was not, and indeed could not have been, "the island of Hinba."

Professor Watson's analysis hinges on the characteristic of the Celtic place-name, already mentioned here, in describing some physical aspect or peculiarity of the landscape, and the fact that the physical geography of Hinba would have remained unchanged even when the name by which Adamnan knew the island was lost to the Norse re-naming of much of the western seaboard. Working from that premise, the first key to the identification of Adamnan's "island of Hinba" is the name by which he calls the site chosen for its community of anchorites in his reference to a holy man who "came over from Ireland and spent the rest of his life in the island of Hinba...having for many years lived without reproach in obedience amongst the brethren, led the life of an anchorite for twelve years more in the hermitage of Muirbolc-mar."

*Muirbolc-mar* — literally "the big sea-bag" — would indicate an unusually large, bag-shaped bay and a feature, incidentally, which is nowhere to be found in the Garvellachs. Hinba, then, lies on the sea-route from Ireland within comfortable reach of Iona and will now have a Norse name, but it must also be an island large enough to accommodate a "big sea-bag," by which feature it can be most securely recognized. One possibility is the island of Colonsay — named from the Norse *Kolbeins ey* or "Kolbein's island" — where there is a bay with a bag-like horn on the shore facing Oronsay, but there is a still more distinct *bolc* formed by a contraction of the sea-inlet of Loch Tarbert which slices up into the west side of the island of Jura, another name deriving from the Norse, *Dyr ey* or "deer island." "The choice," suggests Watson, "seems to lie between Colonsay and Jura" — and to which he adds that "the claims of Jura seem strong."[14] So strong, in the light of all the other evidence from Jura, as to be quite conclusive.

Along the shore of the bag-shaped bay on Loch Tarbert are a number of large caves. One of them is known in the Gaelic as *Uaimh mhuinntir Idhe* or "the cave of the people of Iona," a name which would confirm it, beyond all reasonable doubt, as the site of the "hermitage of Muirbolc-mar." From the point of that recognition, it would seem that the name Hinba itself points firmly to Jura. *Hinba* was Adamnan's Latin form of the Old Irish *inbe,* literally "an incision" and a term which well describes the great cleft of Loch Tarbert cutting Jura almost in half and clearly the original inspiration for the island's Celtic name. To which can be added Professor Watson's discovery of a local tradition calling Jura by the Gaelic name of *an t-Eilean Bán,* "the holy island," and which can only be interpreted as an allusion to an ancient and especial sanctity.

Some similar association may well underlie the Gaelic name of one of the three hills, known collectively since medieval times by the sailor's colloquialism of the

Paps of Jura, which is marked on modern maps as *Beinn Shiantaidh* and most often translated as "the sacred peak." It was Coemgen, the hermit saint of Glendalough, who is said to have called mountains "creatures of God" and the grey quartzite prominences of the Paps of Jura — dominating the view of the island from every prospect and clearly recognizable by their distinctive outline on the south-eastern horizon from the monastery on Iona — do have about them a daunting ascetic quality all of their own.

## The burial-place of Ernan

There are on Jura two especially historically significant "Kil-" dedications and both of them correspond to the evidence of Adamnan's references to Hinba with the most remarkable precision.

Killernandale, anciently *Killernadail,* is a Gaelic-Norse hybrid — the Gaelic *Cill Earnain,* "Ernan's church," suffixed with the Norse *dalr,* "valley" — and the name of the largest, and probably oldest, burial-ground on the island. It was the site of a pre-Reformation church mentioned in Dean Donald Monro's *Description of the Western Isles of Scotland* of 1549 and of the island's parish church until 1777. Whether or not Killernandale was the site of the monastery — for which its situation amidst croftland on the track beyond Keils would have been eminently suitable — its dedication assuredly commemorates Ernan, Columba's uncle appointed prior on Hinba, and may well mark his place of burial.

Adamnan's account of the death of Ernan can be shown to have a useful bearing on the Killernandale dedication on Jura.

The venerable man [Columba] sent Ernan, his
uncle, an aged priest, to preside over the monastery he had founded many years before in Hinba
island. On his departure the saint embraced him
affectionately, blessed him, and then foretold
what would happen to him, saying, "This friend
of mine, who is now going away from me, I never
expect to see alive again in this world." After a
few days this same Ernan became very unwell,
and desired to be taken back to the saint, who
was much rejoiced at his return and set out for
the harbour to meet him. Ernan also himself,
though with feeble step, attempted very boldly,
and without assistance, to walk from the harbour to meet him; but when there was only the
short distance of twenty-four paces between
them, death came suddenly upon him before the
saint could see his face in life, and he breathed
his last as he fell to the ground, that the word of
the saint might be fulfilled.

Hence on that spot, before the door of the kiln,
a cross was raised, and another cross was in like
manner put up where the saint stood at the
moment of Ernan's death, which remaineth until
this day.

Ernan — brother to Columba's mother Eithne who is
commemorated at Kilmeny on Islay — is listed as one
of the twelve men who accompanied the saint to
Scotland. He must by then have been advanced in
years and, consequently, very elderly indeed by the
time of his appointment as prior on Hinba, "a monastery...founded many years before."

Adamnan's chronology is, as always, unhelpful, but
it does contain the clear implication of Hinba being

founded before Iona. He does, however, confirm that
Ernan's time as prior was no more than a matter of
days and also that he died on Iona, but at no point does
he indicate his being buried there. The crosses he
describes mark points associated with Ernan's death,
but not his burial, and if he had been interred on Iona,
Adamnan would undoubtedly have said so. At which
point the narrative is taken up by the local tradition
closely associated with Killernandale and telling of a
holy man "Earnadail" or "Earradail" who had in-
structed that on his death his body should be brought
over from "Islay" to Jura where it was to be borne
along until a cloud of mist appeared to mark the place
where it was to be buried. His instructions were
followed and he was laid to rest in the place indicated
by the prophesied patch of mist, since called Killernandale. The traditional name of *Earnadail* is obviously a
later, post-Norse, corruption of Ernan and "Islay,"
perhaps in the old form of *Ila,* must be most plausibly
interpreted as a misreading of *Ia* for Iona. However
marginally distorted, the tradition still meshes so well
with Adamnan's evidence as to leave little doubt that
the Killernandale dedication marks a site first sanctified by the shrine of Columba's kinsman and still in
use today as a place of burial.

There are some number of memorial carvings to be
seen at Killernandale, ranging from medieval grave-
slabs to the eighteenth-century Campbell mausoleum,
but none of them nearly so old as the crosses etched
into either side of the still more ancient standing stone
placed inside the western wall of another burial-ground
above the bay at Tarbert on the eastern shore of Jura.
The graveyard has no evidence of any burial earlier
than 1800 and its name of Kilmhoire is a dedication to
the Virgin which cannot be earlier than the medieval

centuries, but the sanctity of the site itself is of much
greater antiquity. Within the boundary of the walled
cemetery, but laid out on a quite different alignment
and long covered over with earth, are exposed the
foundations and lower interior walls of a building
usually described as "a Celtic chapel." It is quite clearly
an early Christian site, and one of substantial propor-
tions, but its greatest significance lies in the dedication
contained within its Gaelic name of *Cill Chaluim-chille,*
"Columcille's cell" or "Columcille's church."

## Columba's visions on Hinba

Adamnan's chapters concerning Columba on Hinba
mention a "house" and a "church," which would seem to
have been on the same site, if not contained within the
same building, and that site within reach of a landing-
place from the sea.

For all Adamnan's vague chronology, there is one
chapter which specifically indicates Columba's being on
Hinba after the foundation of Iona, and it has come to
be generally accepted that the saint used the island as
his place of spiritual retreat. The early Christian site
at Tarbert is of sufficient size and proportion to have
accommodated both a monastic cell and an associated
oratory. It is located on the most narrow neck of land
on Jura, above a bay well-suited to a curach landing
and no great distance from the anchorite community at
Muirbolc-mar on Loch Tarbert. There is also, for good
measure, a *Tobair Chaluim-chille,* "Columba's well,"
some little way to the east of the cemetery.

Probability is one thing and proof quite another, but
if it could ever be proven that Cill Chaluim-chille on

Jura was the site of Columba's retreat on Hinba, then
its "Celtic chapel" would have a claim to join the first
rank of eminence among the holy places of the western
sea as the setting for what might be read as the most
sacred chapter of the Adamnan *Life of Columba*.

> When the saint was living in the island of Hin-
> ba, the grace of the Holy Ghost was communi-
> cated to him in matchless abundance and dwelt
> with him in a wonderful manner, so that for
> three whole days and as many nights, without
> either eating or drinking, he allowed no one to
> approach him, and remained confined in a house
> which was filled with heavenly brightness. Yet
> out of that house, through the chinks of the
> doors and keyholes, rays of surpassing brilliancy
> were seen to issue during the night. Certain
> spiritual songs also, which had never been heard
> before, he was heard to sing. He came to see, as
> he allowed in the presence of a very few after-
> wards, many secrets hidden from men since the
> beginning of the world fully revealed; certain
> very obscure and difficult parts of sacred Scrip-
> ture also were made quite plain, and clearer
> than the light to the eye of his pure heart.
>
> He grieved that his beloved disciple, Baithene,
> was not with him, because if he had chanced to
> be beside him during those three days, he would
> have been able to explain from the lips of the
> blessed man mysteries regarding past and future
> ages, unknown to the rest of mankind, and to
> interpret also some passages of the sacred books.
> However, Baithene was then detained by
> contrary winds in the Egean island (Eigg), and
> he was not, therefore, able to be present until

those three days and as many nights of that glorious and indescribable visitation came to a close.

For all that his intention was to demonstrate the outstanding holiness of his saint, there is an illuminating irony in the fact that the chapters in which Adamnan portrays Columba in closest contact with the divine are also those which most clearly reveal his druidic aspect and the visitation of the Holy Ghost over three days and nights on Hinba is one of them. There is an evident parallel between the druid as the man of knowledge with his own élite access to the otherworld and the holy man in solitary retreat to whom are "secrets hidden from men since the beginning of the world fully revealed."

Druidic authority hinged on secrecy. Nothing was committed to writing and the wisdom, lore and learning of the elect was passed orally to each new generation of initiates. For all the transforming impact of Christianity on the spiritual culture of the Irish Celt, there can be no doubt that the holy man was the heir to the druid and nowhere in the early sources is that more evident than in the *Life of Columba*. On the many occasions when Adamnan tells of someone accidentally stumbling upon Columba in contact with angels or surrounded by heavenly light, the inadvertent witness is invariably commanded to say nothing of what he has seen until after the death of the saint. Through the three days and nights of revelation on Hinba, Columba's great regret was the absence of Baithene, his most intimate disciple and intended successor, who was consequently not able to share with him the "mysteries...unknown to the rest of mankind."

Neither were the druidic aspects of the holy man
confined to the realm of the spiritual. Another passage
from Adamnan — again set on Hinba and presented as
an angelic visitation — portrays Columba assuming the
same political role formerly performed by the druid,
that of the king-maker in ancient Celtic Ireland.

In the ritual election of the high-king at Tara, it was
the druid who emerged, wrapped in his cloak of cow-
hide, from a trance of three days duration to announce
the name of the man chosen by the otherworld of the
ancestral dead. So too — on the evidence of Adamnan
— did Columba emerge from his retreat on Jura with
divine authority to ordain the warrior king who was
destined to restore the ascendancy of Scotic Dalriada.

> On another occasion when this eminent man was
> staying on the island of Hinba, he saw, on a
> certain night, in a mental ecstasy, an angel sent
> to him from heaven and holding in his hand a
> book of glass regarding the appointment of
> kings. Having received the book from the hand
> of the angel, the venerable man, at his com-
> mand, began to read it; and when he was reluc-
> tant to appoint Aidan king, as the book directed,
> because he had a greater affection for his bro-
> ther Iogenan, the angel, suddenly stretching out
> his hand, struck the saint with a scourge, the
> livid marks of which remained on his side all the
> days of his life. And the angel added these
> words: "Know for certain," said he, "that I am
> sent to thee by God with this book of glass that,
> in accordance with the words thou hast read
> therein, thou mayest inaugurate Aidan into the
> kingdom; but if thou refuse to obey this com-
> mand, I will strike thee again." When therefore

this angel of the Lord had appeared for three
successive nights, having the same book of glass
in his hand, and had repeated the same commands of the Lord regarding the appointment of
the same king, the saint, in obedience to the
command of the Lord, sailed across to the island
of Iona and there, as he had been commanded,
ordained Aidan, who had arrived at the same
time as the saint, to be king.

Adamnan's powerful account is one of the very few
chapters from his *Life of Columba* which can be precisely dated. The death of Conall mac-Comgall, king of
Dalriada, is entered in the Irish annals at the year 574,
so the ordination of Aidan mac-Gabran as his successor
— and with it, by implication, Columba's vision — can
be securely placed in the same year.

The thirty-year reign of Aidan was of central importance in the history of Celtic Scotland, but there is
evidence in the early sources that his claim on the
kingdom of Dalriada did not go unchallenged and it is
in that context that Columba's vision on Hinba as-
sumes its most historical significance. The Old Irish
genealogies proclaim Aidan to have been the son of
Gabran and thus in direct line of descent from Fergus
Mór, the founding dynast of Scotic Dalriada, yet so too
was his elder brother Iogenan with the greater claim of
seniority and the two sons of Conall with their own
claims on their father's kingdom. There is a cryptic
entry in the annals of one of those sons being killed in
battle on Kintyre and it might have been that the
dispute over the succession erupted into conflict before
Columba intervened with the formidable authority of
his angelic vision.

Much as the druid entered into a trance before

proclaiming a pagan king, it is more than likely that
Columba would have entered upon a regime of solitude,
prayer and fasting to resolve a political crisis. Such
extremes of ascetic practice — producing the state of
mind Adamnan describes as "mental ecstasy" —
induced the visionary experience of the holy man in the
ancient Irish church and such visions were regularly
recruited to underwrite the intervention of the saint in
affairs of state.

Whatever modern interpretations might be placed on
Columba's encounter in retreat on Jura with the angel
bearing the scourge and the book of glass "regarding
the appointment of kings," the decision which it inspired was one of far-reaching importance for the
destiny of the Scottish nation. The eminent modern
historian of early Scotland, Dr Alfred Smyth, describes
Aidan as "one of the greatest warlords in the British
Isles during the early Middle Ages, dominating political
and military events in northern Britain and campaign-
ing from Orkney to the Isle of Man and from Ulster to
Northumbria."[15] If Columba's selection of such a man
for the kingship of Dalriada might be more realistically
ascribed to the political instinct of a holy man descended from warrior kings than to angelic instruction,
then it can certainly be said that history has entirely
borne out the wisdom of his judgement.

The very many references to Aidan which occur in
the Adamnan *Life* confirm a close relationship between
the holy man and the warrior king. Columba is portrayed as Aidan's *anmchara* — literally "soul-friend,"
but effectively spiritual and temporal counsellor —
foretelling the destinies of the king's sons, praying on
Iona for victory in the siege of a hillfort in the Ochils,
and accompanying Aidan in the first year of his reign
to the great council of kings at Drumceat in Derry.

The issues under negotiation at Drumceat are expressed by the early sources in terms of tribute and hosting, the political and military obligations which defined relations between kings and clans in Celtic Ireland, but their resolution amounted to effective recognition of the independence from Ireland of Scotic Dalriada. What was achieved at Drumceat laid the first foundation of what was to become the Scottish nation and if it represented, as it certainly did, the enduring achievement of Aidan's kingship, then it was one which he owed in great measure to the charisma and kinship of Columba.

The saint had come to Drumceat as the patron of two royal houses, the Irish Uí Neill and the Scots Cenél Gabrain. Not only was Columba "soul-friend" to Aidan, but also cousin to the Uí Neill over-king with whom Aidan had to deal, and his arrival, with Baithene and a great company of clerics in train, at the green mound in Derry must have been as impressive as it was dramatic. It was, of course, the first time Columba had set foot in Ireland in more than a decade and the most ancient Irish account of his appearance there describes him wearing a blindfold over his eyes and Scottish turfs bound to his feet that he might neither see nor tread the land of Ireland in acknowledgement of his white martyrdom of exile.

More than two hundred and fifty years after Aidan's triumph at Drumceat another king came out of Argyll to establish a new royal capital on the Tay at "Scone of the high shields." His name was Cináed mac-Alpín, although he is now more familiarly called "Kenneth mac-Alpin," and his historic destiny was the fusion of Gael and Pict into the kingdom of Alba out of which grew the medieval Scottish nation. Kenneth's origins

are at best obscure, but the ancient Gaelic verse
chronicle of the kings of Scots known as the *Prophecy
of Berchan* recognized him as "a son of the clan of
Aidan's son." If indeed he was of the line of Aidan, then
history has confirmed him and his dynasty as the heirs
to Columba's prophetic vision of the angel bearing a
book of glass in the grey shadow of the Paps of Jura.

# The Eucharist of the Abbots

There is one more chapter from the Adamnan *Life* set
on the island of Hinba and which, for all its brevity,
contains so many historical implications for the Celtic
holy man in the Hebrides as to merit close examina-
tion.

It tells of "four holy founders of monasteries" who
came to visit Columba and to share with him the
Eucharist on the island of Hinba.

> Four holy founders of monasteries came from
> Ireland to visit St Columba, and found him in
> the island of Hinba. The names of these distin-
> guished men were Comgell mocu-Aridi, Cainnech
> mocu-Dalon, Brenden mocu-Alti, and Cormac ua-
> Liathain. They all with one consent agreed that
> St Columba should consecrate, in their presence
> in the church, the holy mysteries of the Eucha-
> rist. The saint complied with their express desire
> and entered the church with them on Sunday as
> usual, after the reading of the Gospel; and there,
> during the celebration of the solemn offices of
> the Mass, St Brenden mocu-Alti saw, as he told
> Comgell and Cainnech afterwards, a ball of fire
> like a comet burning very brightly on the head of

Columba while he was standing at the altar and
consecrating the holy oblation, and thus it continued burning and rising upwards like a column, so long as he continued to be engaged in
the same most sacred mysteries.

Three of "these distinguished men" — whose identi-
ties are perhaps somewhat obscured for the modern
reader by Adamnan's use of their clan surnames — are
among the most renowned of all the saints of Ireland
and the fourth of them, if now less well-remembered
than the others, is certainly one of the most interesting.

Adamnan's Comgell mocu-Aridi is best known now as
St Comgall of Bangor, named for his principal foundation on Belfast Lough where its location along the sea-
roads to north Britain, the Hebrides and, especially, to
Gaul and the continent enabled its prominence as
Ireland's great "monastic port." Cainnech mocu-Dalon
is, of course, the same Cainnech who miraculously
recovered on Texa the crozier he had left behind on
Iona. He is most often known as St Cainnech of Aghaboe, the place of his chief Irish foundation which was
to supplant that of Ciaran at Saighir as the royal
church of the kings of Ossory soon after Cainnech's
death in AD 600.

Brenden mocu-Alti is also, like Comgall and Cainnech, often named for his principal church as St
Brendan of Clonfert, but he is still more often and
more popularly known — on account of the medieval
legends which grew up around his extraordinary
seafaring — as "Brendan the Navigator." The fourth
member of Adamnan's quartet of distinguished visitors
to Columba on Hinba was also a voyager saint and one
cast in much the same mould as the more famous

Brendan. Adamnan calls him *Cormac nepos Leathain* — his Latin form of the Irish *Cormac ua-Liatháin,* "Cormac of the race of Liathan" — but his entry in the *Martyrology of Gorman* calls him *Cormac leir,* "Cormac of the Sea." At which point, the historical explanation of Adamnan's account runs into difficulty because, while he is quite unambiguous in describing the visitors to Hinba as "four holy founders of monasteries" and while Comgall, Cainnech and Brendan are well-known by the names of their important Irish foundations, nowhere in any early source, historical or traditional, is there any reference to Cormac as a monastic founder.

The historical Cormac, son of Dimma, is known to have been abbot, perhaps even the first abbot, of the major Irish Columban foundation at Durrow in Offaly, but he was most certainly not its founder and neither is he associated with any other Irish monastery. Nonetheless, if Adamnan says he was the founder of a monastery he must have been so and, because Adamnan's *Life of Columba* drew on predominantly Iona sources, the most probable explanation is that Cormac's monastery was located if not in the Hebrides then in the northern isles. There are the ruins of a tiny chapel dedicated to Cormac on the small island of Eilean Mór lying off Kintyre in the Sound of Jura. While the ruins are known to be medieval and to date back no further than the time of the Lordship of the Isles, the chapel's dedication commemorates Cormac's "cell" which must be the now almost entirely inaccessible cave hermitage at the south end of the island, where a very ancient *Chi-Rho* cross carved on stone was discovered in the last century.

Eilean Mór can be safely identified as Cormac's hermitage, but it is at least unlikely to have been the

site of his monastery. There is another medieval chapel
dedicated to Cormac at Kilmory on Kintyre and looking due west out towards Eilean Mór in the Sound
which would have offered a more plausible monastic
site, but the still greater probability is that Cormac's
monastery lay much further to the north. Adamnan's
accounts of Cormac's search for an ever more remote
"hermitage in the ocean" include a reference to his
voyage to Orkney and it is most likely that Orkney was
in Adamnan's mind when he described Cormac as a
monastic founder.

It was W.F. Skene, the pioneering nineteenth-century historian of Celtic Scotland, who first suggested
that when the four saints "are termed by Adamnan
'founders of monasteries,' he probably means here
monasteries *in Scotland.*" (my italics)[16] Whether or not
Skene was correct in his interpretation of Adamnan's
meaning, there is certainly more than enough evidence
in the early sources to support the substance of his
suggestion.

Brendan, whose obituary is most reliably entered in
the annals at 577, lived into his nineties. He was, thus,
the senior of the four saints and of Columba by more
than thirty years and, beyond any doubt, the first of
them to become a founder of a Hebridean monastery.
Brendan is commemorated by numerous dedications
along the full extent of the western seaboard from
Kerry to St Kilda, plotting the course of the sea-road
which was to take him far out into the North Atlantic,
but what is probably the oldest and certainly the most
informative of the Latin *Lives* of Brendan confirms his
earliest monasteries to have been in the Hebrides and
the first of them established before 524.

[Brendan] came to a certain island of Britain

called Ailech, and there founded a church, pro-
posing to remain there to the end...

There has never been any doubt among scholars in
identifying *Ailech* as the ancient name for Elachnave,
the island monastery of the Garvellach group and the
same island formerly proposed as Adamnan's "Hinba."
The Garvellachs — from the Gaelic *Garbh-eileach,*
"rough rocks" — have all the sea-girt, ascetic aspect
especially characteristic of the Brendan tradition. Not
only is the smaller island beside Elachnave known by
the Gaelic name of *Cúil Bhrianainn,* "Brendan's
Retreat," but the disposition of other "Cill Brendan"
dedications south of Oban point decisively towards the
Garvellachs. Kilbrannan Sound between Arran and
Kintyre is a most unlikely "cell" location, even for a
seafaring saint, and is, in fact, a corruption of the
original Gaelic *Caol Brennain,* "Brendan's Sound," but
the old Kilbrennan place-name near Bridgend at the
head of Loch Indaal on Islay and the Kilbrandon above
the Cuan Ferry on the Isle of Seil would suggest two
perfectly plausible hermitage sites along his progress
to Elachnave. Brendan's disciples formed the core of a
monastic community which survived on the Garvellachs
until at least the eighth century — on the evidence of
the "beehive" cells dated by archaeologists to some two
hundred years after Brendan's time — but the saint
himself was not, in the event, able to fulfill his intention "to remain there to the end."

The explanation of a holy man's abandoning his
voluntary exile and returning to Ireland presented
something of a problem to the authors of *Lives* of the
saints and for the best of hagiographical reasons,
because the pursuit of the white martyrdom was, in
principle, an act of aspiration. The saint could decide to

undertake a pilgrimage for Christ outside the land of Ireland but his achievement of permanent exile, the actual white martyrdom, was an act of divine grace in reward and recognition of his sanctity. Thus Columba, who suffered exile for the greater part of his adult life and whose place of resurrection lay far beyond Ireland, represented the ideal of the white martyrdom. Other "pilgrims for Christ," for whatever true reason, had to return to their homeland and, consequently, their hagiographers needed to find some form of explanation of the circumstances which did not diminish the holiness of their saints.

The *Life of Cainnech,* for example, tells how the saint resisted appeals from "the saints of Ireland" until he was finally "brought back from his hermitage against his will," but the Latin *Life of Brendan* offers a far stranger tale of saints and sea monsters to explain Brendan's decision to abandon his exile on the Garvel-lachs.

The holy man "was on a lofty crag in this island when he saw two sea monsters coming from the depth of the sea and fighting desperately together, each of them trying to drown the other." As one creature began to win supremacy, its unfortunate rival called in desperation — and "with a human voice" — upon the protection of the saints of Ireland, first on "St Patrick, Chief-Bishop of the Irish," then on "St Brendan, here present," but all, apparently, to no avail. Only when the drowning monster called upon the name of "the holy virgin, St Brigid" did the attacker desist and "Brendan marvelled greatly at this" and felt it necessary to return to Ireland and ask of Brigid "why such monsters of the deep had more fear of her than of other saints." The precise form of Brigid's reply varies from manuscript to manuscript, but the substance of her explanation is the same in them all, as it is in the closely similar episode included in her own Irish *Life:* while Brendan thinks sometimes of worldly things, Brigid's thoughts are never, not even for a moment, diverted from God.

"Monsters of the deep" — representing mythologized forms of the species of whale, dolphin and porpoise still to be seen, if less frequently now than in antiquity, in Hebridean waters — appear elsewhere in the early sources for sea-going saints as they do in later Gaelic tradition, and it would be no great feat of zoological imagination to propose Brendan's duelling "sea-monsters" as a killer whale in pursuit of a porpoise. The spiritual significance of the exchange between the two saints must have some bearing on Brendan's special relationship with the whale which features prominently in the legendary accounts of his later voyaging, but it is its historical significance for his early career which is of immediate importance here.

An encounter between Brendan, who was born around 486, and Brigid, who lived until 524, is entirely plausible and all the more so by reason of Brigid's being closely associated with Brendan's foster-father, St Erc of Slane (d. 512). If the meeting between the two saints is remotely historical — and scholars generally accept it as such — it would place Brendan's return to Ireland at some point before February 1st, the date on which Brigid's festival is entered in the calendars of saints, in the year 524. He must, therefore, have founded his monastery on the Garvellachs at some point before that date and at least forty years before Columba left Ireland.

The date of Brendan's second Hebridean foundation is still less certain, although it was earlier than the foundation of his principal Irish church at Clonfert around 561, but the evidence of the Latin *Life* leaves no doubt of its island location.

> St Brendan set out again for Britain and
> founded a church there, called Bledach in the
> region that is named Heth, and there worked
> many miracles.

"Heth regio" in the Latin *Life of Brendan* and "Ethica terra" in the *Life of Columba* represent Latin translations of the Old Irish *tír Iath,* "land of Eth," from which is derived the modern island name of Tiree. A large island, twelve miles long and lying out in the Atlantic some twenty miles west of Mull, Tiree has long been famous for its arable fertility and, throughout the Age of Saints, appears to have served as the "monastic granary" of the western sea. Brendan's foundation, very probably intended to serve as a supply base for his Atlantic voyages, may well have been the first of at least four monasteries known to have been established on Tiree by the second half of the sixth century.

It is more than likely that Cainnech of Aghaboe established a hermitage, if not a monastery, on the island, if the place-name dedication of Cillcainnech is of greater antiquity than the ruined medieval church which stands today at Kilkenneth on Tiree. The *Life of Cainnech* mentions two island names — Ibdone and Eninis, "island of the birds" — in association with the saint's time in the Hebrides and, while neither can be firmly identified, one of them must represent the old name of Inchkenneth lying just a mile off the shore of the Isle of Mull.

Known to Fordun in the fourteenth century as *insula sancti Kennethy* and described by Dean Monro in the sixteenth century as "a fair ile, fertill and fruitfull,"

Inchkenneth is a sloping green slab of an island, just a mile long and half a mile wide, in the sea-inlet of Loch na Keal, "the loch of the churches," where it slices into the west side of Mull. The ruins of monastic buildings which greatly impressed Johnson and Boswell when they stayed on the island in 1773 are all that now remain of what must have been a substantial medieval monastery on the site of Cainnech's earlier foundation.

St Comgall is said to have nurtured an early ambition to seek the white martyrdom in Scotland, but was advised against such a course and, in the event, chose Bangor in Down as the site of his first monastery and principal church.

It was not until some time after his foundation of Bangor that Comgall had occasion to visit the Hebrides and the events and circumstances of what seems to have been his only "pilgrimage to Britain" are detailed in the *Life of Comgall*.

> In the seventh year after the monastery of Bangor had been founded, the holy father Comgall sailed to Britain, wishing to visit certain saints there, and to remain there for a time. And he founded a monastery there, in a certain village in the region of Heth and there he remained for a while.

In the course of the saint's stay on Tiree, "a number of heathen plunderers from the Picts came to that village to carry away everything that was there, whether man or beast."

It might be interesting to mention here the particular association of Tiree with the proto-Pictish pirates of the western and northern isles who were mythologized in Irish tradition as the Fomoire sea-demons. It was this same Iron Age culture, very probably descended from the Bronze Age settlement of the western sea-board, which raised the dry-stone built circular towers since called "brochs," from the Norse *borg* or "fortress." Archaeologists have uncovered the remains of some five brochs on Tiree, which indicates the island as a significant centre of the broch culture and corresponds impressively with the evidence of an ancient Irish poem in praise of the semi-legendary king Labraid Loing-seach of the second century BC who "destroyed eight towers in Tir Iath."

More than seven centuries after Labraid's assault on Tiree, Comgall proved himself no less accomplished in dealing with piratical Picts when he called down divine retribution on the raiders who "carried off to their ship the brethren of Comgall and all their substance."

> Worshipping the Lord, he signed the sky and the earth and the sea; and immediately the heathen were struck with blindness, and the sea swelled dreadfully so that it cast the ships upon the shore and the bodies of the heathen were severely injured. Then they abandoned all that they had taken and with earnest prayers begged for pardon from St Comgall; and the saint, moved with pity, prayed for them. And they recovered their eyesight and calm was restored, and they returned, empty and enfeebled.
>
> Afterwards St Comgall was conducted back to Ireland by many holy men.

The especial historical value of the *Life of Comgall* here lies in its evidence, deriving from a tradition entirely independent of Iona, for two episodes which

are also included in Adamnan's *Life of Columba*. When
the evidence of both these sources is brought together
and due allowance made for each one's hagiographical
intentions, it might be possible to set the Eucharist of
the five holy men on Hinba into its true historical
context.

The *Life of Comgall* indicates the saint making just one
journey to Scotland, states its purpose as being "to visit
certain saints there," and places it "in the seventh year
after the foundation of the monastery at Bangor."
While the date of the foundation of Bangor is variously
entered between 553 and 559 in the Irish annals, the
most reliable entry is that found in the *Annals of
Tigernach* under the year 557. The seventh year after
557 would place Comgall in Scotland around 564.

Adamnan's account of Columba's visit to the Pictish
high-king, Bruide mac-Maelchon, at the hillfort of
Craig Phadrig near Inverness makes no mention of any
other holy man going there with him, but the *Life of
Comgall* names both Comgall and Cainnech as Columba's companions and apportions equally among the
three saints those same miracles which Adamnan
credits to Columba alone.

> On one occasion three most blessed abbots, St
> Comgall, St Columba and St Cainnech, came to
> the heathen king called Bruide; and the king
> commanded the doors of the fortress to be shut
> against them. But St Comgall broke the gates
> with the sign of the holy cross and they fell bro-
> ken to the ground; and St Columba broke the
> door of the king's house with the same sign, and
> St Cainnech also signed the king's hand which
> was flourishing a sword to slay them. And imme-

diately the king's hand was dried up and so remained until he believed in God.

The true purpose of Columba's long and difficult
journey to Craig Phadrig was clearly more than the
conversion of a high-king, if indeed that formed any
part of his intention. It was, without any doubt at all,
a mission of diplomacy in the course of which Columba
secured the authority of Bruide for the foundation of a
monastery on Iona. Following Comgall's recent encounter with Pictish piracy, it would be no less realistic to
propose his purpose at Craig Phadrig, and that of
Cainnech also, as the negotiation of similar assurances
for their monasteries in what was, after all, territory
only recently subjugated by the Picts.

Another holy man, who was certainly not present at
Bruide's fortress is, nonetheless, confirmed by Adamnan to have been a beneficiary of Columba's negotiations with the high-king of Picts.

> "Some of our brethren have lately set sail and
> are anxious to discover a desert in the pathless
> sea; should they happen, after many wanderings,
> to come to the Orkney islands, do thou carefully
> instruct this chief, whose hostages are in thy
> hand, that no evil befall them within his domin-
> ions." The saint took care to give this direction,
> because he knew that after a few months Cor-
> mac would arrive at the Orcades.

If it is not too speculative to imagine that the safe
conduct for "some of our brethren...anxious to discover
a desert in the pathless sea" was negotiated for the
benefit of Brendan as well as his fellow-voyager Cormac, it might be possible now to throw some genuinely

historical light on Adamnan's account of the Eucharist on the island of Hinba.

The geography of the matter is swiftly resolved when Hinba is identified as Jura, the more so if the Cill Chaluim-chille at Tarbert does, in fact, mark the site of Columba's cell. Comgall's journey from Tiree to Ireland — on which the *Life* confirms he was accompanied "by many holy men" — would have followed much the same course as Cainnech's voyage to Texa, passing down the west side of Jura, but turning into Loch Tarbert instead of pressing south into the Sound of Islay. The chronology is still more secure when Comgall's only visit to Scotland is placed in the year 564 which is the date widely accepted by scholars for Columba's visit to Bruide.

A delegation of holy men coming together to challenge a high-king with wonder-working and collective charisma occurs more than once in the sources for early Christian Ireland and, if the real purpose of the meeting of four Irish abbots with Columba on Jura had been to prepare a political mission to the royal capital of Pictland, it would have followed in just the same tradition.

For Adamnan the hagiographer, writing some hundred and twenty-five years after the event, the significance of the episode centred on the "ball of fire like a comet burning very brightly on the head of Columba." It could only be interpreted as a sign from heaven, all the more impressive for its occurrence in the midst of such distinguished saintly company, of the outstanding holiness of his saint, but the original reason for the preservation of the story in Iona tradition may, in fact, have been quite different.

When the incident is set into its historical context, the celebration of the Eucharist might be interpreted as an invocation of heavenly blessing on their mission and on its objectives. Comgall and Cainnech were seeking security for their island monasteries. Brendan was probably hoping for the same, but also — and like Cormac — in need of a safe conduct for his curachs soon to be on voyage through the Outer Hebrides and Orkney in search of a hermitage in the ocean.

Columba, whose royal lineage would naturally have placed him at the head of the company, was seeking to achieve a still more historic purpose at Craig Phadrig. His mission was to secure the sanction of the Pictish over-king for the foundation of the monastery destined to become the first royal church of the kingdom of the Scots on the island which was to enter the history of Celtic Scotland as *I-Columcille.*

# IONA
# "I-Columcille"

It was always characteristic of the Irish Celt to endow almost every river and hill, offshore island and standing stone he saw around him with its own legend of his ancestors and forbears, thus investing the whole landscape of Celtic Ireland with the mythic history of his gods and heroes.

That same pagan enthusiasm seems to have been quite undiminished by the impact of Christianity, if only on the evidence of the earliest *Life* of Patrick — that set down by Tírechán in the mid-sixth century — which is largely taken up with a list of places where it claims the saint had founded churches, wells beside which he had prayed, and rivers he had crossed, blessed or cursed. The profusion of place-name dedications throughout the Hebrides shows the same custom to have followed the progress of the saints of Ireland into the western sea, and there the outstanding example of the Celtic identification of holy man with holy place is the island which is still called in the Gaelic *I Chaluim Chille,* "Iona of Columcille."

# The holy island of the western sea

When the layers of medieval legend, later Gaelic folklore, and modern mysticism are peeled away, the pre-eminence of Iona among the holy places of the Hebrides rests entirely upon its historical association with the greatest saint of the Gael. It was on this tiny island — just three miles long and nowhere more than a mile wide — lying off the Ross of Mull that Columba founded the principal church of his white martyrdom, yet neither he nor any of his successor abbots would have known the island by that name.

The name Iona appears nowhere in the sources until the mid-sixteenth century and apparently originated as an error on the part of a late medieval scribe. Adamnan knew the island on which he was abbot for twenty-five years as *Ioua insula,* "the island of Iou," from which — suggests Professor W.J. Watson — "by a misreading of *u* as *n* has come the popular form *Iona*. It is likely that the error gained currency, if it did not originate, from a remark of Adamnan on Columba's name, which he says is in Hebrew *Iona* (Jonah), a dove."[17] Adamnan's *Iou* — or, possibly, *Io* — appears elsewhere in the earliest sources as *Hii, Eo, Ia,* or simply *I* and re-emerges in medieval usage, conjoined with the name of the founding saint, as "Hycolmbkill" in Fordun, "Ycomekill" in the *Register of the Great Seal of Scotland,* and elsewhere in other variant forms of *I-Columcille.* The same name-form was still current at the end of the eighteenth century when the locally-informed *Statistical Account of Scotland* insisted in 1798 that the island "is always called I, except when the speaker would wish to lay special emphasis upon the word, then it is called Icolmkill."

Perhaps not quite "always," on the evidence of Dr Samuel Johnson's account of his Hebridean travels, written a full quarter of a century before the *Statistical Account.* It is true that both Johnson and his companion, James Boswell, use the name "Icolmkill," but the good Doctor's most oft-quoted reference to the island declares his little envy for the man "whose piety would not grow warmer among the ruins of Iona" and it may very well have been those famous words which have done more than anything else to popularize the use of the latter name-form.

If Columba might have not immediately recognized Dr Johnson's name for his island, he would certainly not have recognized the "ruins of Iona" by which were meant the roofless remains of the Benedictine foundation established and endowed by the medieval Lordship of the Isles. The most ancient building on Iona today — as, indeed, in Johnson's time, although much restored since then — is the twelfth-century "St Oran's Chapel."

There was an historical Odhran, the saint whose feast is entered in the calendars under October 27th and whose obituary is entered in the *Annals of the Four Masters* at 548, a full fifteen years before Columba left Ireland. There are place-name dedications which, if they are of sufficiently genuine antiquity, indicate his having been in the southern Hebrides, but the tradition linking him with Iona, like the chapel which bears his name, can be traced back no further than the twelfth century.

While some portions of the ruins of the medieval Nunnery are as old as the thirteenth century, most of them are dated to as much as two hundred years later. The present Iona Cathedral is an almost entirely twentieth-century restoration of ruins which may well have stood on the site of the Columban oratory, but were themselves fourteenth-century fragments of the Benedictine abbey church. Even the great stone-carved standing crosses on Iona, none of them surviving intact, are products — as is the Kildalton Cross on Islay — of the later eighth century, some two hundred years after the death of the founding saint.

There are, of course, a number of sites on Iona which can be genuinely identified with those mentioned by Adamnan's *Life of Columba.* The late Iron Age hillfort, now known by the tautologous Gaelic-Norse name of *Dùn Bhuirg* ("fort fort"), above the north-west shore is his *Munitio magna,* or "Great fortress," where he tells of Columba's watching the passage of a "pestilential cloud." The green, rounded hill where Columba met with angels is the same one called in the Gaelic *Sìthean mor,* or the "great fairy mound" — with all the otherworld associations from the Irish tradition of the *sídh* which that name implies. The part-artificial miniature hill immediately to the west of the present Cathedral is nowadays known as *Tor Abb,* "hillock of the abbot," and with every authenticity when its size and situation correspond precisely with Adamnan's references to Columba's cell. All of which are unchanging natural features rather than monumental remains and so it might still be said that nothing tangible — other than sections of the *vallum,* the earth-worked rampart which marked out the perimeter of the monastic site — remains of the original sixth-century foundation.

From another perspective, however, the Iona of Columba's time can be brought into sharp historical focus. It is that perspective which is of central interest here and it might be best described as "a view to the sea."

On Iona, as nowhere else throughout all his dominions, one especially evocative line from an ancient bardic description of Columba preserved by Manus O'Donnell in his *Betha Colaim Chille,* is made vividly clear.

> Abbot of churches which a great wave
> reaches...

Adamnan mentions just two monasteries founded in Scotland by Columba and both of them can be seen from Iona.

Away to the south, the unmistakable cloven outline of the Paps of Jura marks out Hinba, "the island of the cleft," on which Columba founded the first monastery church of his white martyrdom. Looking out to the westward, the island of Tiree is too low-lying to be as distinctly obvious as Jura, but can still be seen on the horizon beyond the rolling Atlantic breakers. Following the example of Brendan and Comgall, Columba also established a monastic foundation on Tiree, which he would have known by Adamnan's name of *Ethica terra,* "the (is)land of Eth," and placed it for a time under the supervision of his fosterling and successor, Baithene. It is known to have included its own community of penitents, who would have been employed there as farmworkers, because the Columban foundation on Tiree — called by Adamnan *campus Lunge,* his Latin

form of the Irish *mag Lunge,* "the plain of the ship" —
was, in all practical essentials, an arable farm, intended to supply the granary of the parent foundation
on Iona. It might even be possible to locate *mag Lunge*
close to Tiree's main village of Scarinish on the evidence of a document of 1592 included in the *Register of
the Great Seal of Scotland* and concerning lands "at
Skervenis in the island of Tyree...which formerly were
part of the patrimony of abbots of Y Comekill."

# Iona in Dalriada

It is possible, then, to walk no great distance on Iona
and see all of the historical Columba's Scottish foundations, remaining at the same time within view of the
site of his principal church.

So too, the view to the northward from Dun I, the
highest hill on Iona, can take in the full extent — from
the Ross of Mull to the peaks of Skye — of the historical Columba's central area of activity in Scotland, an
area which — when expressed in terms of the political
geography of the sixth century — indicates his pastoral
circuit to have been concentrated, as was his principal
monastery located, within the territory of the Cenél
Loairn.

The ancient "clan of Loarn" are believed to have been
settled in Argyll generations before Fergus mac-Erc
arrived to claim his kingdom in 498 and their lands,
centred on the capital fortress of Dunollie at Oban and
extending outward from the Firth of Lorn — which
name commemorates, by inference, their eponymous
founding dynast — represented the most northerly
extent of the early settlement of "the Irish in Britain."
Their territories were, thus, ranged at such hazard

along the frontier of Dalriada as to have inevitably suffered first and most grievously from the Pictish onslaught of 560. If the annalist's entry of "the flight of the Scots before Bruide mac-Maelchon, king of Picts" refers, as it surely does, to the clan of Loarn, then their territory — including Iona — must have been effectively lost or, at best, survived as "debatable land" by the time of Columba's arrival from Ireland in 563.

When Columba's choice of Jura for his first foundation in Scotland is placed into that political context, its logic becomes clear. Jura was, first of all, an island and, thus, in the tradition of the Celtic church a place especially suited for a monastery in its being set apart from the secular world by divinely-appointed waters. It was an island of ascetic aspect and yet endowed with sufficient fertility and resources for a sizeable monastic community to be self-supporting. Most important of all in a time of the iron sword, it was securely situated within the heartland of Dalriada, no great distance across the Sound from the hillfort of Dunaverty and some way to the south of Dunadd. The situation of Iona was quite different and the foundation of his monastery there confirms the dramatic impact of Columba on the political balance between Pict and Scot.

There is at the southern end of Iona — above the bay called *Port a churraich,* "Bay of the Curach," which tradition claims to have been the site of Columba's first landing on the island — a heap of stones known as *Cárn cùl ri Eirinn,* "Cairn of the Back to Ireland." A still more dubious tradition explains the cairn as marking the place from which the saint looked back to ensure he could no longer see his homeland from the island on which he was to found his church. Unfortunately for that doubtful tradition, not only is it sometimes possible — given exceptional visibility — to make

out the Irish coast from that viewpoint, but there is
another cairn of the same name no great distance away
on Mull. That "Cairn of the Back to Ireland" stands on
a neck of land near Ben More where there is also a
*Càrn cùl ri Albainn,* "Cairn of the Back to Alba" and
suggests a more historical explanation of the names as
marking points on the frontier of the Irish settlement
of western Scotland. The Cárn cùl ri Eirinn on Iona,
then, serves most plausibly to locate the island in a
disputed borderland and to propose Columba's foundation there of his principal church as a dramatic advance in the restoration of the kingdom of Scotic
Dalriada.

For all the historical importance of the foundation of
Iona, there is no account of it anywhere in the earliest
reliable sources, least of all in Adamnan's *Life of
Columba,* and neither is its date reliably entered in any
Irish annal. Bede's date of 565 is so very plausible as
to be widely accepted, but is still not entirely beyond
dispute and all that can be said with absolute assur-
ance is that the monastery had been established by the
year 574. Both the *Annals of Ulster* and those of
Tigernach enter the obituary of Conall mac-Comgall,
king of Dalriada, at that year and add to it a note of
Conall's having gifted Iona to Columcille. Adamnan
fully supports their evidence when he confirms Columba to have been on Iona to consecrate Aidan mac-
Gabran as Conall's successor. The territorial implications of that ceremony of succession being conducted on
Iona hardly need any further explanation, but there
can be no doubt of the political significance of Columba's principal church as the bedrock on which the new
ascendancy of Scotic Dalriada was to be raised by
Gabran's son, "king of Alba."

From that point in history, the destiny of the Dalriadic kingdom was bound up with that of the Columban church and it was a bond underwritten as much by geography as by the political alliance between the royal houses of the Cenél Gabrain and Uí Neill, because the dominions of Columba and those of Aidan were ranged along much the same extent of the western seaboard. As the monastic *familia* of the ancient Irish church corresponded to the tribal *túath* of secular Celtic Ireland, so too did the principal church of a founding abbot correspond to the capital fortress of a warrior king. I-Columcille, for all its foundation on piety and learning, represented a power base for a holy man born of warlord stock.

# The evidence of Adamnan

The idea of Iona as a remote island monastery is entirely modern and no less misleading. It is an island, surrounded on one side by the often dangerous currents of the Sound and on the other by the great expanse of the Atlantic, but it is only remote from the viewpoint of a culture, itself arguably a legacy of the Roman occupation of Britain, long centred on towns and cities linked by roads. The same sea which presented a barrier to the Romans served the Celt of the west, as it had his forbears through three millennia of prehistory, as his great thoroughfare of settlement, trade and warfare.

Iona stood at the centre of a monastic network extending from Durrow to Tiree in its founding saint's own lifetime and still further in the time of his successor abbots, a *paruchia* which was linked, of necessity, by sea. With that thought in mind and remembering that Adamnan was himself abbot of the same island monastery served in its every need by the sea, it is hardly surprising that the sea should be everywhere in his *Life of Columba.*

Even Adamnan himself recognized how often he describes visitors to Iona announcing their arrival at the shore on the Ross of Mull by "shouting across the Sound."

> A loud cry was heard beyond the above-men-
> tioned Sound of which I speak so often. As soon
> as the saint heard it, he said to the brethren
> who were then with him, "Go directly and bring
> here before us at once the strangers that have
> now arrived from a distant land." They went
> accordingly and ferried the strangers across...

The Sound of Iona seems often to serve the monastery as an outer range of the monastic vallum, barring access — as it did while the monks conducted the funeral rites for their founding saint — in response to divine command of wind and wave.

> God was pleased at his [Columba's] prayer to
> quell the storms and to calm the seas; and
> again, when he found it necessary, as on the
> occasion [of the burial] just mentioned, the gales
> of wind arose as he wished and the sea was
> lashed into fury; and this storm, as hath been
> said, was immediately, so soon as his funeral
> rites were performed, changed into a great calm.

For an abbot of Iona, the sea was as much a source of anxiety as of supply and communication. On the 16th of September 691 — while Adamnan was still at work on his *Life* of the founding saint — "a great gale drowned six of the community of I[on]a" — according to an entry in the *Annals of Ulster* at that year. Visiting holy men from Ireland, such as the abbot mentioned earlier at hazard in Brecan's whirlpool, were regular beneficiaries of Columba's command of storms at sea in ensuring their safe passage and island-going brethren were assisted in their voyages to different destinations by his timely direction of changing winds. Sea-crossings between the islands are regularly mentioned, most often between Jura, Tiree and Iona, but on one occasion Adamnan refers to Baithene being detained by unfavourable winds on Eigg, an island monastery outwith the Columban *paruchia* and to be considered here later in another context. Columba is regularly portrayed watching from a high point on the island for the approach of craft from Ireland, sending messages there by evidently regular curach traffic and, on one occasion, receiving news from the continent when a Gaulish wineship put into Kintyre. Adamnan's revelation of maritime information is inevitably more accidental than intentional and there is only one occasion when he indicates much technical detail. It must be said, though, that those details are of seafaring in his own time, a full hundred years after Columba. He refers, for example, on occasion to "sailors," implying professional mariners rather than sea-going monks and who may have formed a part of the lay personnel attached to the monastery. These seamen were undoubtedly employed in Adamnan's time and later, being mentioned by the annals in connection with at least one travelling abbot in the eighth century, but that does not confirm that they were employed in the monastic seafaring of a century earlier, and it is quite probable that they were not.

One aspect of monastic seafaring, as characteristic of Adamnan's time as of Columba's and even of Patrick's, was the extensive use of the hide-hulled curach, effectively the same skin-boat in use on the western sea since the Bronze Age and before, but Adamnan also confirms the construction, at least in his own later seventh century, of planked vessels, perhaps akin to the Gaulish wineship.

> On the first occasion we had to draw over land
> long boats of hewn pine and oak, and to bring
> home in the same way a large quantity of mate-
> rials for building ships.

It was, nonetheless, the curach which was especially associated with the holy man at sea and Adamnan indicates its serving a variety of purposes. In the same chapter quoted above, for example, he describes a fleet of curachs bringing a cargo of timber for monastic building on Iona.

> On the second occasion, which was a few years
> after the one just mentioned, our monastery was
> requiring repairs, and some oak trees were to be
> taken from near the mouth of the river Sale [the
> Shiel in Moidart], in twelve vessels which we
> brought for the purpose.

From the variety of references to the curach — in Adamnan as elsewhere in the early sources — it is reasonable to infer a variety of such craft, from the smallest, crewed by six or eight oarsmen and well suited for service as a ferry across the Sound, to the large ocean-going sailing curach capable, as was no other vessel until the viking longship, of north Atlantic voyaging.

# Iona on the sea-road

To touch on the great theme of seafaring saints in the northern ocean is almost immediately to move out of the orbit of Columba of Iona and into that of his elder contemporary, Brendan the Voyager, and in so doing to highlight the strategic situation of Iona on the "sea-road of the saints." Iona is the point on the sea-road beyond which everything seems suddenly to change. It is the point beyond which the early sources of history seem to be engulfed in a flood tide of legend, "founders of monasteries" are overtaken by "hermits of the ocean," and the pursuit of the "white martyrdom of exile" is transformed into the quest for the "Land of Promise of the Saints."

It might be said that Columba's diplomatic mission to the high-king of Picts was of two-fold importance to the course of the history of the holy man in the Hebrides, first of all in securing Iona for his own monastic power base. It may have been that had he never left Ireland, his eminence and lineage alone would have marked out his principal monastery as a greatly influential foundation, but his titanic personal charisma still further enhanced by his impressive achievement of the white martyrdom lent I-Columcille a stature virtually unrivalled in the ancient Irish church. It would seem, and not only from Adamnan's evidence, almost as if a constant traffic plied between Ireland and Iona to create a great marine thoroughfare described in Irish tradition as "a bridge of curachs."

The further importance of Iona on the sea-road was already in evidence in Adamnan's account of Columba's negotiations with the high-king of Picts. While there must have been some number of securities sought and gained from Bruide by the three saints who came to his fortress at Craig Phadrig, the only one specifically identified by Adamnan was the safe-conduct arranged by Columba for Cormac who "had gone far from land over the boundless ocean at full sail...to discover a desert place in the ocean."

It was not Cormac's only such voyage, because Adamnan mentions two more, and neither was Cormac the only holy man to sail in search of an ocean hermitage. Adamnan names only one other, a Baitan who is known from no other source, but there is a wealth of evidence throughout the sources for very many more. Neither is it realistic to imagine the "safe conduct" as applying exclusively to Cormac and his companions, who are described to Bruide only in the most general terms as "some of our brethren [who] have lately set sail...to discover a desert in the pathless sea." It would have held good, in effect, for any seafaring holy men claiming an association with Iona and Columba on voyage throughout Bruide's dominions of the northern and western isles. That probability, taken together with Adamnan's reference to Columba's name being "proclaimed in every province of the isles of the ocean," points firmly to Iona as the great monastic port for the hermits of the ocean and, consequently, the principal forward base for what Tim Severin has called "a Christian sea-going culture which sent boat after boat into the North Atlantic on regular voyages of communication and exploration."[18]

Perhaps the bardic author of a quatrain included in the Irish *Life of Columcille* was describing just that same "sea-going culture," because of all the hundreds of thousands, even millions, of words written about Iona through thirteen hundred years, I can think of none which evoke its place on the sea-road of the saints so well as his.

> Wondrous the warriors who abode in Hy,
> Thrice fifty in the monastic rule,
> With their curachs along the main sea,
> Three score men a-rowing.

There is every likelihood that the modern jetty on Iona stands on much the same site as the one Adamnan knew as "the landing place on the Iouan island." Very many sea miles separate that landing place from the most northerly hermitage of the Hebrides on the distant isle of North Rona, traditionally so named for a holy man called Ronan, and it may be purely accidental that the jetty on Iona is known in the Gaelic as *Port Ronain,* "St Ronan's Bay."

# THE OUTER HEBRIDES AND BEYOND

# "In Search of a Hermitage in the Ocean"

Some few years before 1870, Alexander Carmichael made the acquaintance of Angus Gunn of Ness in the north of the Isle of Lewis, a man who has been called "one of the last great storytellers, a treasure-house of history and legend."[19] It was from Gunn that Carmichael learned the story, which he afterwards included in his *Carmina Gadelica* collection of Gaelic tradition, of the strange voyage of the holy man Ronan to his hermitage in the ocean on the back of the sea creature *cionaran-crò*.

Ronan came to Lewis to convert the people to
the Christian faith. He built himself a prayer-
house at Eorabay [now Europie in Ness, Isle of
Lewis]. But the people were bad and and they
would not give him peace. The men quarrelled
about everything, and the women quarrelled
about nothing, and Ronan was distressed and
could not say his prayers for their clamour.

He prayed to be removed from the people of
Eorabay, and immediately an angel came and
told him to go down to the landing-rock, where
the *cionaran-crò* cragen was awaiting him.
Ronan arose and hurried down to the sea-shore,
shaking the dust of Eorabay off his feet, and
taking nothing but his satchel, containing the
Book, on his breast.

And there, stretched along the rock, was the
great *cionaran-crò,* his great eyes shining like
two stars of night. Ronan sat on the back of the
*cionaran-crò* and it flew with him over the sea,
usually wild as the mountains, now smooth as
the plains, and in the winkling of two eyes
reached the remote isle of the ocean. Ronan
landed on the island, and that was the land full
of biting adders, taloned griffins, poisonous
snakes and roaring lions. All the beasts of the
island fled before the holy Ronan and rushed
backwards over the rocks into the sea.

And that is how the rocks of the island of
Roney are grooved and scratched and lined with
the claws and the nails of the unholy creatures.
The good Ronan built himself a prayer-house in
the island where he could say his prayers in
peace.

The island of "Roney" is the same "remote isle of the ocean" lying forty-four miles north-north-east of the Butt of Lewis and known since the 1850s as "North" Rona — to distinguish it from the more southerly isles, one of them off Raasay and the other off Benbecula, of the same name — but neither the saint nor his sea monster are to be identified with any such precision. Which species of great whale might have been mythologized by the Gael as the *cionaran-crò* is quite unknown, although the name does occur elsewhere in Hebridean tradition where it was tentatively suggested by Carmichael as the Gaelic equivalent of the legendary kraken. The holy man Ronan should be more easily identified than his *cionaran-crò* and, indeed, would be were there not so many saints of that name entered in the calendars.

There are four Ronans in the seventh-century *Martyrology of Oengus* and eight more in the twelfth-century *Martyrology of Gorman*. Another, described as a "bishop" of Kingarth on Bute, is commemorated on February 7th in the Scottish calendars but nowhere in the Irish, although his obituary is entered by the *Annals of Ulster* at 737. Bede's *Historia Ecclesiastica* mentions "one particularly vigorous champion of the true [i.e. Roman] Easter, named Ronan, [who] was Irish by race" disputing with Bishop Finan of Lindisfarne in the mid-seventh century, but Bede's Ronan can be no more securely identified with any one of his name in the calendars than can the Ronan of Angus Gunn's story.

There is, nonetheless, firm archaeological evidence for the presence of a holy man on Rona at least as early as the eighth century. It takes the form of an ancient carved stone shaped into a rudimentary cross (now removed to Lewis for its greater safety) and the stone-built remains of a hermit's cell adjoining the crumbled walls of a twelfth-century extension which was confidently identified in 1549 by Dean Donald Monro's *Description of the Western Isles of Scotland* as "ane chapell callit St Ronans Chapell." It would seem likely that the Ronan of that dedication is the same saint commemorated at Europie in the north of Lewis, where nothing other than a few stones around a green mound remains of another *Teampull Ronain,* "Ronan's Chapel," and, by inference, also the man for whom the island of Rona itself was named, were it not for serious doubt as to whether the island name derives from a dedication to a saint at all.

North Rona is known to naturalists as one of the most populous breeding grounds of the Atlantic grey seal, whose Gaelic name of *ròn* might suggest "Seal Island" as the origin of the name. Against which must be weighed the predominance of Norse-derived nomenclature in the Western Isles and the consequently greater probability of the old form of Roney having originated as the Norse *hraun-ey,* "the rough isle," in recognition of the precipitous cliffs ranged along its rugged eastern shore.

It might, then, be reasonable to imagine a medieval cleric, some few hundred years before Dean Monro, recognizing a Norse-derived Roney as an old dedication to any one of a number of Ronans he had encountered in the calendars and, perhaps, translating that erroneous connection into a sermon which was to eventually re-emerge, encrusted with elements out of still more ancient tradition, as the legend Alexander Carmichael learned from Angus Gunn. One of the leading authorities on the early sources of history, J.F. Kenney, offers a stern warning regarding the historical reliability of legend:

> Legend belongs to the realm of folklore, where
> the transmission of facts is exceedingly erratic.
> The folk mind sometimes retains the record of
> an event with extraordinary accuracy from gen-
> eration to generation, sometimes within a few
> years distorts it beyond recognition. It is a me-
> dium which cannot be trusted.[20]

Not least in the Outer Hebrides, where it can take no
more than a single generation to transform historical
record into folk legend. The discovery of the twelfth-
century ivory chess pieces, since known as the "Lewis
Chessmen," by an islander "digging a sandbank" on the
western shore of the island for which they were named
was reported in a Scottish newspaper of June 1831, yet
a gothic tale of storm, shipwreck, murder and plunder
to explain the find was already current in Lewis by
1863. The tradition of a coast where the folklore
gestation period need be no more than thirty years
presents the historian of the ancient Irish church with
a vast expanse of perilously thin ice. Whatever might
have once been genuinely traditional recollections of
the holy men who sought their hermitages in the ocean
in the Western Isles more than twelve centuries ago
have been very largely obscured by the legacy of
medieval whimsy which put saints to sea on slabs of
stone for the sole purpose of contriving a spurious
"relic."

The historical record of those who chose for their
retreats the most remote islands of the western sea is
inevitably fragmentary, if only because *Lives* of saints
were the products of scribes working in the great
monastic communities and it would be at least imprac-
tical to imagine a *scriptorium* such as that on Iona in
the windswept isolation of North Rona. Nonetheless,

fragments of reference and allusion to holy men in search of a hermitage in the ocean did find their way into the early sources and the evidence of those fragments, taken together with that of archaeology and reliable tradition, can leave no shadow of doubt as to the powerful attraction of sea-girt solitude for the ancient Irish church.

# Hermits of the ocean

From Skellig Michael off the coast of Kerry, where the remains of a monastic settlement still cling to the vertiginous rock seven hundred feet above the Atlantic, to Sula Sgeir, "the gannets' rock" where a ruined cell inspired Angus Gunn's story of Ronan's sister who found solitude ten miles west by south of Rona, it would seem that almost no island along the full extent of the western seaboard proved too remote or inaccessible for the Irish holy man. The early sources customarily describe such islands as "deserts in the ocean," implying that they provided the monks of the west with their equivalent to the desert hermitages of the Egyptian pioneers of the monastic idea, and it would seem that island foundations were characteristic of Irish monasticism from its very beginnings. St Enda of Aran was a junior contemporary of Patrick and also, according to tradition, spiritual counsellor to Brendan the Voyager. He has been described by one eminent authority as "the earliest organizer of Irish monasticism"[21] and his choice of the isolated Aran Islands off the coast of Galway as the site of his own foundation in the late fifth century initiated a tradition of island monasteries which was to follow the saints of Ireland into the Hebrides.

The extension of that tradition into the quest for a "hermitage in the ocean" is usually, and very plausibly, explained as a retreat from a major monastery being drawn into ever closer contact with the secular world, but it might also reflect the response of the Celtic holy man to the Hebrides themselves. Reaching out into the ocean north and west of Skye, the Outer Hebrides — or the Western Isles to use their more resonant modern name — offer a prospect quite unlike that of the islands south of Skye. In the context of Dark Age Scotland they lay far beyond the frontier of Dalriadic territory along a seaboard which had even then been a pirate coast for some thousand years. They were quite different also — then as now and most importantly here — in their geology and the Irish Celt was always highly sensitive to landscape.

The Western Isles are largely formed, as is the island of Iona, of Lewisian gneiss, some of the oldest rock of all the earth's crust. There is no way of knowing whether a holy man out of early Christian Ireland had any recognition of that geological antiquity, although it would seem that his druidic forbears were able to seek out the oldest rocks for their holy places, but neither is it necessary to understand modern earth sciences in order to sense the extraordinary quality of permanence which characterizes the Outer Hebridean landscape, the awesome drama of its gales and storms, or the magical quality of its ever-changing light. Set against mountains carved from rock that was made in the beginning of the world, the presence of humankind on these islands seems at no time other than precariously fragile. For a holy man intending to set himself apart from the transient concerns of men, his senses honed by extremes of self-denial and his mind focussed on the eternity of the divine, these far-flung fastnesses of the western sea must have offered their own uniquely impressive spiritual significance.

If a place can be found within that context for the fragmentary evidence preserved in the early sources, it might, perhaps, be possible to reclaim from the tenacious clutches of legend at least something of the historical reality of the search for a "desert in the ocean."

# Beccan of Rhum

The earliest reference by name to a Hebridean hermit — or at least the earliest I have been able to find — occurs in a letter already mentioned in these pages.

It is that written around the year 632 by Cummian, abbot of Durrow, to Segine, abbot of Iona, and concerning the question of the dating of Easter. The content of Cummian's letter has already been discussed and is of less significance at this point than the name of one of those to whom it is addressed:

> [To] Segine, successor of St Columba and other holy men, and to Beccan the solitary, his dear brother according to the flesh and in the spirit, with his wise companions.

Beccan, a monk of the Columban *paruchia* and brother to the learned abbot of Durrow, was a "solitary" — *solitario* in Cummian's Latin dative form and perhaps better translated as "anchorite" — and the place of his solitude is entered with his obituary in the *Annals of Tigernach* at the year 677.

> Beccan of Rhum reposed in the island of Britain.

The large island of Rhum, approximately eight miles square and dominated by its own massive Coolin, lies between Canna and Eigg and some eight miles to the south-west of Skye. It cannot be strictly included among the "Outer" Hebrides, but in the political geography of early seventh-century Scotland it did lie at the northern extremity of Irish settlement and within the orbit of the proto-Pictish "broch culture." If its community of anchorites — comparable, perhaps, to the one at Muirbolc-mar on Jura — can be accounted "hermits of the ocean," then Cummian's letter copied to "Beccan the solitary...with his wise companions" can claim to be the first contemporary documentary record identifying any one of those who found "a desert place" in the western sea. It can also be taken as a genuinely historical indication of the esteem in which such anchorites were held, when Beccan — and with him, by implication, "his wise companions" — was evidently considered of a sufficient intellectual stature to merit inclusion in an exchange between eminent churchmen on a crucial question of theology.

# Cormac of the Sea

A full six decades separate Cummian's letter from the next early source to make reference by name to another anchorite, this one, perhaps, closer in character to Brendan of Clonfert than to Beccan of Rhum. The chapters of Adamnan's *Life of Columba* concerning the voyages of the holy man remembered as "Cormac of the Sea" are the earliest and most substantial historical record of what has come to be known as the "voyage tradition" of the early Irish church. For all the wide celebrity of Brendan, there is no surviving account of his voyages which can be dated to within two hundred years of Adamnan's chapters on Cormac and, for that reason alone, they are deserving of some close attention here.

Other than the evidence of Adamnan, all that is known of the historical Cormac ua-Liathan derives from his entries in the Irish martyrologies under his feast-day of June 21st. His surname confirms his people to have been the *Uí Liathain,* "the race of Liathan," whose tribal territory lay on the coast of Cork, and his father Dimma was a nobleman of that clan. His evocative title of *Cormac leir,* "Cormac of the Sea," occurs in the *Martyrology of Gorman* where his entry goes on to describe him as "abbot of Durrow and...also an anchorite." The *Martyrology of Oengus* records his place of burial as "Durrow of Columcille," but no annalist enters his obituary and the most probable date of 590 derives only from the best-informed speculation of modern historians.

For all that his interest in Cormac is confined to illustrating the powers of his own saint, Adamnan is much more forthcoming on the subject than any martyrologist and the sixth chapter of the first book of his *Life of Columba* is entitled "Of Cormac"...

Columba prophesied in the following manner of Cormac ua-Liathain, a truly pious man, who not less than three times went in search of a desert in the ocean, but did not find it:

"In his desire to find a desert, Cormac is this day, for the second time, now embarking from that district which lies at the other side of the river Moda (the Moy in Sligo) and is called Eirros Domno (Erris in Mayo); nor even this time shall he find what he seeks, and that for no other fault than that he has irregularly allowed to accompany him in the voyage a monk who is going away from his own proper abbot without obtaining his consent."

Those two paragraphs offer a valuable insight into the spiritual aspect of the search for "a desert in the ocean" and, by implication also, into that of the whole Christian voyage tradition. Like the pursuit of the white martyrdom of exile, the quest for a hermitage in the ocean was an act of aspiration and the fulfillment of such aspiration in arrival at the divinely-appointed "desert" hinged not at all, it would seem, upon seamanship, survival or navigational skills, but upon the saintliness of the aspirant and the exemplary holiness of every aspect of his voyage. Thus Adamnan explains Cormac's being denied the object of his quest for no other reason than divine disapproval of one of his companions having neglected to secure the permission of his abbot, an oversight of which Cormac himself knew nothing.

There is, in fact, a discernible note of disapproval in both of Adamnan's accounts of Cormac and it can be reasonably taken to reflect his relationship with Columba, a theme taken up by later medieval sources informed by Irish tradition. Cormac is everywhere portrayed as an attractive personality — "a fair cleric" according to Oengus — and Columba evidently held him in such high regard as to insist on his appointment as abbot of the important foundation at Durrow. Cormac, for his part, was reluctant to accept even so prestigious an office if it required him to abandon his voyaging and that conflict between aspiration and obedience brought about a recurrent, but still apparently good-natured, dispute between the two saints.

Their dispute is dramatized by an Irish verse dialogue composed in the tenth or eleventh century, but informed by a tradition of still greater antiquity. Just one quatrain, placed in the voice of Columcille, from that source is sufficient to illustrate the style and substance of his dispute with Cormac of the Sea:

> Though thou travel the world over,
> East, west, south, ebb, flood,
> Thou noble son of high-born Dimma,
> It is in Durrow thy resurrection shall be.

If the same tradition had been known to Adamnan, as it well might have been, it is difficult to imagine his interpreting Cormac's reluctance as other than a monk's disobedience to his abbot and, thus, just cause for the failure of "not less than three" attempts "to find a desert."

From Adamnan's perspective, then, the course of a voyage in search of a "desert in the ocean" was a matter of divine dispensation and, consequently, his passing references to point of departure, direction or landfall occur as merely accidental details, few in number and always tantalisingly insufficient for the historian's purposes. In the chapter quoted above, for example, Adamnan notes Cormac setting sail from the north-west coast of Mayo, but there is no further indication of the course of his voyage or its duration.

The second voyage described by Adamnan is one to which reference has already been made here in connection with Columba's arrangement of a safe conduct from the high-king of Picts for Cormac's company "should they happen, after many wanderings, to come to the Orcadian islands." There is no note of the starting point of this voyage, but its duration is specified as being of "a few months," in which time Cormac "had gone far from land over the boundless ocean at full sail" and evidently, in the light of his expected landfall on Orkney, some distance into the north Atlantic. What Adamnan's evidence does make clear, however, is that Orkney was a landfall made en route — and, by implication, on the return journey — but not the hoped-for "desert in the ocean." The fact that Columba's request for the safe conduct was made "because he knew that after a few months Cormac would arrive at the Orcades," would suggest Orkney as a customary landfall for such seafaring monks and later evidence will confirm that it continued to be so until the end of the eighth century.

There is every likelihood, then, that some form of Irish monastic settlement was established on Orkney as early as the mid-sixth century, perhaps no more than clusters of cells and not necessarily permanently occupied, but certainly available as forward bases for voyagers in search of a hermitage in the ocean. A number of Orcadian locations have been suggested as likely sites of such foundations, most prominent among them the sea-girt outcrop of the Brough of Deerness on the north-east tip of the Orkney mainland.

Linked only precariously to the shore by boulders washed by the waves of the North Sea, it has every aspect of a typically "Celtic" site, so much so as to have been described by eminent archaeologists as "an excellent example of a Celtic monastery." It is difficult to imagine anywhere more suitable to accommodate what might be imagined as Cormac's foundation, yet the remains of a chapel and monastic buildings on the Brough of Deerness — as, indeed, elsewhere in Orkney — "are unlikely to be pre-Norse" in the view of its most recent archaeological investigators who have found no conclusive evidence of an Irish Celtic presence.[22] It would seem that Adamnan's acknowledgement of Cormac as a "holy founder of monasteries" must remain an enigma still unresolved.

Having omitted identification of Cormac's point of departure for his "second attempt to discover a desert in the ocean," Adamnan does, at least, indicate his port of return as having been Iona and it would seem most likely that it was also the home port for the third and most extraordinary of the voyages attempted by Cormac of the Sea.

Having mentioned thus briefly the prediction of the blessed man regarding Cormac's second voyage, we have now to relate another equally remarkable instance of the holy man's prophetic knowledge regarding his third voyage.

While Cormac was laboriously engaged in his third voyage over the ocean, he was exposed to the most imminent danger of death. For, when for fourteen days in summer and as many nights, his vessel sailed with full sails before a south wind, in a straight course from land, into the northern regions, his voyage seemed to be extended beyond the limits of human wanderings, and return to be impossible.

Accordingly, after the tenth hour of the fourteenth day, certain dangers of a most formidable and almost insurmountable kind presented themselves. A multitude of loathsome and annoying insects, such as had never been seen before, covered the sea in swarms, and struck the keel and sides, the prow and stern of the vessel, so very violently that it seemed as if they would wholly penetrate the leathern covering of

the ship. According to the accounts given afterwards by those who were there, they were about
the size of frogs; they could swim, but were not
able to fly; their sting was extremely painful,
and they crowded upon the handles of the oars.

When Cormac and his fellow-voyagers had
seen these and other monsters, which it is not
now our province to describe, they were filled
with fear and alarm and, shedding copious tears,
they prayed to God, who is a kind and ready
helper of those who are in trouble. At the same
hour our holy Columba, although far away in
body, was present in spirit with Cormac in the
ship. Accordingly he gave the signal, and calling
the brethren to the oratory, he entered the
church, and addressing those who were present,
he uttered the following prophecy in his usual
manner:

"Brethren, pray with all your usual fervour for
Cormac, who by sailing too far hath passed the
bounds of human enterprise and is exposed at
this moment to dreadful alarm and fright in the
presence of monsters which were never before
seen and are almost indescribable. We ought,
therefore, to sympathize with our brethren and
associates who are in such immediate danger
and to pray to the Lord with them; behold at
this moment Cormac and his sailors are shedding copious tears, and praying with intense
fervour to Christ; let us assist them by our prayers, that God may take compassion upon us, and
cause the wind, which for the past fourteen days
has blown from the south, to blow from the
north, and this north wind will, of course, deliver
Cormac's vessel out of all danger."

Having said this he knelt before the altar and, in a plaintive voice, poured forth his prayers to the almighty power of God, who governeth the winds and all things. After having prayed he arose quickly and, wiping away his tears, joyfully gave thanks to God, saying, "Now, brethren, let us congratulate our dear friends for whom we have been praying, for God will now change the south into a north wind, which will free them from their perils and bring them to us here again." As he spoke the south wind ceased and a north wind blew for many days after, so that Cormac's ship was enabled to gain the land. And Cormac hastened to visit Columba, and in God's bounty they looked on each other again face to face, to the extreme joy and wonder of all.

Adamnan's only note of his source of information is the reference to "accounts given afterwards by those who were there," which can only mean reminiscences preserved for at least a hundred years in the oral tradition of Iona, and it would seem that tales of terror have always been especially susceptible to elaboration in the retelling. Nonetheless, Adamnan's vivid account of Cormac's curach under assault by denizens of the deep can be shown to have made a deep impression on hagiographers who came after him, not least the twelfth-century Irish *Life of Brendan* from the *Book of Lismore* which includes an almost identical episode presented as a vision of Hell revealed to Brendan amid wild Atlantic seas and most generously described as "inspired" by Adamnan's original.

The most plausible source of Adamnan's story, then, is an amalgam of tales brought back to Iona by Cormac and his companions of their various encounters with unfamiliar wildlife in northern seas. The "multitude of loathsome and annoying insects [which] covered the sea in swarms [and] crowded upon the handles of the oars" have been suggested as "sea nettles," a form of jelly fish called "live drops" in the Western Isles where they have been known to form themselves into a glutinous mud on keels and the blades of oars and to cluster so densely in the water as to make it appear almost solid. The "other monsters, which it is not now our province to describe" can be taken, as can the *cionaran-crò,* to refer to any number of unfamiliar species of great fish and cetaceans abounding in the most northerly Atlantic, because there is no doubt that Cormac's "straight course from land, into the northern regions...beyond the limits of human wanderings" had led him some distance into the Arctic seas beyond which lay those regions known in antiquity as Thule.

The earliest references to "the (is)land of Thule" derive from Pytheas' account of his voyage of 300 BC, in the course of which he claimed to have sighted a northern land lying some six days' voyage from the north of Britain and another day's sailing from "the frozen sea." The classical geographers who incorporated the evidence of Pytheas into their own work preserved the report of his sighting of Thule, but without any very precise indication of its whereabouts.

It is believed now that the Thule reported by Pytheas was one of the uninhabited islands off the west coast of Norway. It is no less likely that the land sighted by Agricola's naval expedition round the northern coast of Britain in the later first century AD and reported to have been Pytheas' Thule would have been the Fair Isle north of Orkney or Foula west of Shetland, if it was not, in fact, Sumburgh Head at the southern tip of Shetland itself.

Whichever region was identified by Pytheas or the Romans who came after him as Thule, it is least likely to have been Iceland, yet the land known as Thule in the Irish sources — whose authors had, of course, discovered the name from classical geographers — certainly was Iceland, which may have lain beyond the operational range of Roman warships but is known to have been well within reach of Irish holy men in their oceangoing curachs. One such was an immediate contemporary of both Cormac and Columba and a holy man especially associated with the Outer Hebrides, although his principal church lay on the island off Morvern for which he is entered in the calendars as Moluag of Lismore.

# Moluag of Lismore

There is no surviving *Life* of Moluag. Neither is there any record in the early sources of the date of the foundation of his monastery on the long, grassy island in the sea-loch Linnhe and while tradition places it at 562, it could well have been as much as a decade earlier. What can be said with every confidence is that the saint did not sail to Lismore on a stone and neither did he race against Columba to win the island for himself by cutting off his finger to cast ashore ahead of his rival, both of which are claims made for him by his less plausible traditions. If he was of Uí Neill lineage, as one genealogy claims, it would have been unlikely that he was the monk of Bangor which another tradition suggests, and all that is really known of the historical Moluag is the obituary entered in the *Annals of Tigernach* at 592.

> The death of Lugaid of Lismore, that is, Moluoc.

From which it would appear that *Moluoc,* the form of Moluag used by Tigernach and the older martyrologists, was an affectionate form — *Mo-Luoc,* "my Lugaid" — of his real name. His entry under June 25th in the *Martyrology of Oengus* is typical of the warm esteem with which he is commemorated in the Irish calendars.

> The pure, the bright, the pleasant,
> the sun of Lismore;
> that is Moluoc,
> of Lismore in Alba.

Even if many dedications to "my Lugaid" are as likely to be of medieval origin as survivals from the saint's own time, they are still sufficiently numerous to rank Moluag among the most popular of Scotland's saints and many of their locations correspond impressively to historical probability. The two Kilmoluag place-names on Kintyre — one of them looking out towards the Oa on Islay and the other across the sound to Jura — are well-placed for the customary sea-road from the north of Ireland. So also, the Kilmoluag dedications on Mull, on Tiree, on Raasay, and near Uig on Skye as well as that on Lismore itself, would indicate a sphere of activity centred on his principal church.

Of special interest here, though, are two further-flung dedications in the Western Isles. There is a Kilmoluag on Pabbay — one of many similar island

names deriving from the Norse and indicating an "isle
of the priests" — in the Sound of Harris and a *Teampull Mholuig*, "Moluag's Chapel," at Europie in Ness,
the most northerly parish on the Isle of Lewis. If that
dedication to Moluag is of genuine antiquity — and
there is a distinct probability of its being so — then it
can claim for him the singular distinction of the most
northerly commemoration of an historically identifiable
saint in the Hebridean archipelago.

The sea-road which took the saints of Ireland into
the Arctic ocean led them there, inevitably, by way of
the Western Isles and it would be no wild speculation
to suggest the northern tip of Lewis as another likely
forward base for the holy man seeking a hermitage in
the ocean. So too, on the evidence of the course taken
by Cormac's second voyage, was Orkney, and Orcadian
tradition offers an interesting, if tenuous, association of
Moluag with the tiny island of Papa Westray, another
Norse "priest isle" place-name.

However fragile they might be considered, the
associations of Moluag of Lismore with Lewis and
Orkney do serve to underwrite an old tradition entered
in the *Breviary of Aberdeen* which, first of all, estab-
lishes Moluag as a pupil of "the blessed abbot Brandan"
and goes on to claim that, after his foundation of
Lismore, "he then went to Thule..."

All of which must point to the possibility, if no more
than that, of Moluag of Lismore having sailed with
Brendan of Clonfert, but there would seem to have
been no saint associated with northern seafaring whose
tradition has not been drawn into the orbit of the
extraordinary Brendan the Voyager, because — as J.F.
Kenney explains — "it was around the figure of Brendan that the lore and the romance of this extraordinary
phase of the history of the sea coalesced."[23]

# Brendan the Voyager

While there has never been any question of the historicality of Brendan of Clonfert, the tradition of "Brendan the Navigator" has been often unjustly relegated to the wilder shores of legend. Nonetheless, the relationship between history and legend surrounding this extraordinary saint has always been as complex as it can be shown to be revealing.

The Brendan sources are, in every essential, variants of two different texts, both of which are believed to have derived from a common original, long since lost. Of these two principal sources, the *Navigatio Sancti Brendani Abbatis,* "The Voyage of St Brendan the Abbot," has been proposed as the more ancient. It is preserved in some hundred and twenty surviving manuscripts, the oldest of them dated to the tenth century, but even that is a copy — set down in Ireland by an Irishman — of an earlier exemplar.

The *Navigatio* has been called "the Odyssey of the Irish church"[24] and its roots lie deep in the most ancient tradition of the Celts of the west. It is also an historical source of the greatest importance for the searoad of the saints, but it is exclusively concerned with Brendan's voyaging in search of "the Land of Promise of the Saints" and so contains no account of his lineage, churches, or indeed almost anything of his life before the eve of his embarkation. Consequently, the search for the historical saint must look beyond his voyage tradition to the other body of Brendan sources comprising his Latin and Irish *Lives* and from which, in conjunction with the Irish annals, can be assembled an outline of his biography.

"Brendan, son of Findlug...of the Ciarraige Luachra"

was born — according to his Irish Life — "in the time
of Oengus, son of Nad Fraech, king of Munster." The
obituary of Oengus, king of Munster, is entered at 490,
a date which would fully concur with the entry of the
saint's birth at the year 486 in the *Annals of Innis-*
*fallen,* an eleventh-century Munster compilation
considered an especially reliable authority for the
historical Brendan. His birthplace was long held to be
Fenit near Tralee town, but modern scholarship has
shown Annagh — beneath the Slieve Mish mountains
rising up from the southern shore of the Bay of Tralee
where the sagas tell of Finn mac-Cumaill and his
warband racing their horses on the sand — to have the
stronger claim. There is, at least, no doubt of Brendan's
being a Kerryman from the Dingle Peninsula — the
clan country of his people of the Ciarraige Luachra, for
whom the county of Kerry is named — where he is
commemorated by a profusion of place-names, Mount
Brandon, Brandon Head, Brandon Bay and Brandon
Peak amongst them.

The *Lives* are all agreed that he was ordained into
the priesthood by St Erc of Slane, who was probably
also responsible for fostering the young Brendan.
Consequently, the date of his ordination must be placed
before 512 — the year at which Erc's obituary is
entered in the *Annals of Ulster* — when Brendan would
have been a man in his later twenties.

> When Brendan had been ordained a priest by St
> Erc, he then received the holy habit of a monk;
> and many persons, forsaking the world, came to
> him from various directions.

On the evidence of his Latin *Life,* the date of Brendan's
first monastic foundation — at Ardfert, a few miles

north-west of Tralee — can be placed shortly after his ordination and as much as a decade before his departure from Ireland to seek the white martyrdom of exile in the Hebrides, which is probably what is intended by the reference in the Irish *Life* to his seeking "the secret, retired, secure retreat in the ocean, far apart from mankind." Something of the history of Brendan's first Hebridean foundation, the island monastery of Ailech on the Garvellachs, has already been explored here and with it the evidence for his return to Ireland at some time before the death of Brigid in February 524 (see p. 120).

At which point, any attempt to impose a chronology on the evidence of the Brendan sources becomes entangled with his voyage tradition and it is not until the foundation of his principal church at Clonfert, entered by the *Annals of Innisfallen* at 561, that Brendan the Voyager can be reclaimed by history from the realm of legend. He would have been already in his seventies by the time of his foundation of Clonfert — *Clúain ferta Brénaind*, "Brendan's meadow of the graves" — and, very sensibly, retired from his more ambitious seafaring. Even in his last decades, Brendan the Voyager seems not to have submitted to inactivity. Adamnan confirms him to have been on Jura with Cormac, Comgall and Cainnech in 564, when the vision of "a ball of fire burning very brightly on the head of Columba" was revealed to Brendan alone, and the Latin *Life* describes his travelling extensively on pastoral circuits of Munster up until his death at Clonfert, which is entered under May 16th in the calendars and at the year 577 in the *Annals of Ulster*.

Whatever might have been the true duration of Brendan's "seven years upon the sea"[25] in search of the

Land of Promise of the Saints, the evidence of the early
sources can place it no more precisely into the Brendan
chronology than within a time span bounded by his
return to Ireland from the Garvellachs and his foundation of Clonfert almost forty years later.

All the *Lives* of Brendan make reference to his
voyage tradition — the Irish *Betha Brenainn* in the
form of a lyrical synopsis probably originating as a
homily for his feast day and the Latin *Vita Brendani* in
its choice of chapters introduced as incidents occurring
"when St Brendan was on his voyages on the ocean" —
but the most detailed narrative account of Brendan's
seafaring is to be found in the Latin *Navigatio Sancti
Brendani Abbatis*.

The *Navigatio* narrative begins with the visit to
Ardfert of "a certain father called Barinthus (a Latin
form of the Irish *Barrfind)* of the line of Niall," who
tells of having sailed "to the west, towards the island
called the Land of Promise of the Saints which God will
grant to those who succeed us in the latter days...a
land spacious and grassy, and bearing all manner of
fruits." Inspired by Barinthus to go himself in search of
the Land of Promise, Brendan selects fourteen monks
from the community of Ardfert as his companion
voyagers. Together they make the necessary spiritual
and practical preparations, including the construction
of the leather boat in which they "set sail towards the
summer solstice."

Their first landfall is providential in appearing just
as their supplies reach the point of exhaustion and
brings them ashore on "an island rocky and steep,"
apparently uninhabited but in fact occupied by an
anonymous young man who provides them with food,
drink, and supplies to continue their voyage. They sail
on to the "Sheep Island" where they stay from Maundy

Thursday to Easter Saturday taking prophetic guidance from another enigmatic island monk described as "the venerable procurator" to whom they return each year as the Easter festival approaches. Easter Day itself is spent on what appears to be a nearby island, but is, in fact, a great whale to which they return each year on the anniversary of the Resurrection. They sail on to another neighbouring island, described as the "Paradise of Birds," and afterwards to many more islands, each of them occupied by its own solitary hermit or even a monastic community. Such is the one found on the "Island of St Ailbe," where Brendan's company celebrates the first Christmas of its voyage and returns each Christmas to stay until Epiphany with the shipwrecked survivors of Ailbe's community.

The voyage — or, more accurately, voyages, because Brendan seems to have been engaged on seven annual circuits of the north Atlantic — is thus laid out in accordance with the church calendar. It includes visionary encounters — one of them with Judas Iscariot, clinging to a sea-girt rock on a day's relief from the torments of Hell and another revealing the pit of Hell in the chasm beneath a great wave — which have been shown to have originated as sermons delivered by Brendan on voyage. There are also reports of sightings of "wonders of the ocean," amongst them the "Island of the Smiths" with its forges casting fire on the sea and a towering "column of the clearest crystal which seemed to pierce the skies," recognizable now as natural phenomena rendered in similarly visionary form. Eventually, after seven years of voyaging, Brendan and his companions pass through "a dense cloud so dark that they could scarce see one another," beyond which they come at last to the Land of Promise of the Saints, before the *Navigatio* concludes with an unex-

pectedly summary statement of the saint's return to
Ireland.

It must be clear from even so brief an outline of its
narrative that the *Navigatio* was intended as a spiritual text, which might appear to offer little of value to
the historian. There are no recognizable place-names
after the saint has departed the shores of Kerry, and
almost every indication of duration and distance is
expressed in terms chosen for their scriptural or
numerological significance. The numbers "three,"
"seven" and "twelve" are qualified by their biblical
associations as well as magical import inherited from
Celtic tradition, but "forty days" can only be taken to
mean "a very long time."

All of which must have lent weight to scholarly
dismissal of Brendan's voyage tradition as Christian
myth, one commanding greater respect by virtue of its
quality and antiquity than fanciful fictions claiming
saints crossing the sea on stones, but a myth nonetheless. The most generous assessment of the *Navigatio*
was, until relatively recently, that of those Celtic
scholars who recognized it as the outstanding Christian
reworking of the *immram*, the "voyage to the otherworld" of ancient Irish tradition, described by Kenney
as "a type of pagan romance which itself must have
sprung from the folklore of the maritime peoples of
Ireland who for unknown ages had looked out upon the
mystery of the broad Atlantic."[26]

The sea has long held a powerful spiritual significance for the Celt of the west, his thoroughfare of
prehistoric antiquity and his way to the pre-Christian
otherworld of Tír na n-Og beyond the setting of all the
suns. The *Voyage of Bran* — telling of a man lured
across the sea to an island paradise by the Túatha Dé
Danann and having passed into the otherworld finding

himself beyond hope of return to Ireland — is considered the best-preserved, if inevitably retouched, survival from the pre-Christian voyage tradition. Just as folk-memories of prehistoric seafaring nourished the deepest roots of the sea-road of the saints, so other surviving *immrama* texts have been convincingly proposed as pagan originals drastically recast into Christian form, but the *Navigatio Sancti Brendani Abbatis* can be shown to be very much more than that.

While its form does correspond to that of the immram, such a correspondence might amount to no more than a convenient literary device and especially when the twelfth-century *Book of Leinster* included the *immram* in its list of the "prime stories" of bardic tradition. Form is one thing, content quite another and it is the historical implication of the content of the *Navigatio* which is of central importance here.

There is really only one outstanding candidate for the first rank of Brendan scholarship in recent decades and he is Tim Severin, whose bold approach to the content of the *Navigatio* has most impressively demonstrated its genuine significance for the historian of the ancient Irish church.

Dr Severin's own account of his work, published under the title of *The Brendan Voyage,* is too well-known to need further recommendation here, but it might be helpful to consider his research and findings before directing their light on to the Outer Hebrides. Severin set out to test the premise that the voyage indicated by the *Navigatio* could have followed a "stepping stone route" across the Atlantic to reach continental North America a thousand years before its "official" discovery by Christopher Columbus. To do so he needed a seaworthy sixth-century curach and no

trace of such a craft — constructed, after all, of eminently biodegradable wood and skin — has survived to
be uncovered by the archaeologist's spade.

There are illustrations of leather boats down the
ages, but just one closely contemporary illustration of
the oceangoing craft of the Age of Saints. It is carved in
low relief on an eighth-century stone cross-shaft at
Bantry in Cork, crusted with lichen and so badly worn
over twelve hundred years that the image of a craft
crewed by four oarsmen and a more prominent figure
with a steering oar beneath a cross mounted on its
stern-post, is only just discernible. The craft is evidently a skin-boat with the same lifting lines of the
bow evident in the Kerry curragh of more recent times
and its four oarsmen, rowing rather than sculling, can
be taken to represent a crew of twice that number. It
is a true sailing vessel built with a keel and capable of
deep seagoing, its hide-hulled buoyancy enabling it to
ride lightly with Atlantic waves which might easily
overwhelm a weightier wooden vessel.

It was just such a vessel as this, mentioned throughout the early sources but represented in greatly simpli-
fied outline by an early medieval religious artist, which
had to be realized for the "Brendan Voyage." To that
end, Severin commissioned Irish craftsmen informed by
traditional expertise handed down through uncounted
generations to construct a vessel from the same materials and on the same principles described with remarkable technical precision in the second chapter of the
*Navigatio:*

> St Brendan and his companions, using iron im-
> plements, prepared a curach, with wooden sides
> and ribs, such as is usually made in that coun-
> try, and covered it with cow-hide tanned in oak-

bark, tarring the joints thereof, and put on board
provisions for forty days, with butter enough to
dress hides for covering the boat, and all utensils
needed for the use of the crew.

Severin's finished vessel — 36 feet overall with an 8-
foot beam, oak keel and gunwhales, a hull formed of
ox-hides stretched over an ash frame, driven by a
mainsail and foresail hung from its two masts and 12-
foot oars — was as precise a replica as could be accomplished by painstaking craftsmanship and meticulous
research of the craft which occurs throughout the
documentary record of the sea-road of the saints.[27] His
*Brendan* was, in every verifiable particular other than
its VHF radio-mast, the same leather boat in which
Columba had made his "pilgrimage to Britain," Cormac
had sought his "desert in the ocean," and, most importantly, in which Brendan the Voyager had put to sea in
search of the Land of Promise of the Saints.

Severin's course was laid from the coast of Kerry in
the shadow of Mount Brandon, up the west coast of
Ireland, north to Iona and on through the Hebridean
archipelago by way of the Minches. By passing, thus, to
the east of the Uists, Harris and Lewis he would have
missed sighting the distinctive profiles of the group of
Hebridean outliers marked on modern maps as St
Kilda. There is no "Kilda" entered in any calendar of
saints and the name is believed now to have originated
as a misreading by a sixteenth-century cartographer.
The evacuation of its last community of islanders in
1930 brought to an end a record of human settlement
which had endured on St Kilda since the Bronze Age.
On the largest of the group, the island known by the
Norse-derived name of Hirta, are ruined cell-type
structures at least as old as the early Christian period

and it is unimaginable that these islands would have
been overlooked by those who sought a hermitage in
the ocean.

There is also on Hirta a chapel dedication to Brendan. It is customarily and casually described as "post-
Norse," whatever that might mean, but Brendan
dedications are untypical of the contexts of the two
other dedications on the island — one a "Christchurch"
of likely Orkney-Norse origin and the other a characteristically medieval commemoration of Columcille. I
have seen no more of St Kilda than its outline on the
horizon looking west from North Uist, but that sighting
did suggest a cautious correspondence with the evidence of the *Navigatio,* which implies Brendan's first
landfall lying some way to the west of the Outer
Hebrides. He was twelve days out from Kerry when a
fair wind dropped to a sudden calm and his monks
resorted to the oars "until their strength was nearly
exhausted." They had lost all sense of direction and
their provisions were spent, when "there appeared
towards the north an island very rocky and steep."
They negotiated a landing with difficulty and were
rewarded with hospitality from an unnamed, enigmatic,
but evidently well-supplied, solitary holy man. To
suggest that first landfall as St Kilda would, of course,
be pure speculation.

Dr Severin's course had carried him out into the north
Atlantic before he began his identification of the
islands described by the *Navigatio.*

The "Sheep Islands" were the Faeroes, a name
deriving from the Norse *Faer-eyjaer* and translating,
almost too obviously, as "Sheep Islands." Severin
identifies one of two other islands of the Faeroe group,
Mykines or Vagar, as the "Paradise of the Birds." There

Brendan's monks heard the birds singing psalms, but only the saint himself was able to understand the voice of the bird which perched on the prow of his boat, explaining that its companions are "fallen angels" and advising Brendan on the future course of his voyage.

Perhaps the *Navigatio* is here offering its own mystical allusion to the importance of observed bird behaviour to ancient navigators. The Old Testament tells of Noah releasing first a raven and later a dove from the Ark in the hope of their discovering land uncovered by the abating Flood, until the dove's failure to return from its third flight confirms for him that "the waters were dried up from the earth." It is a story which was borrowed by the Book of Genesis from a still older Babylonian legend and akin to others found in ancient traditions from Persia to the Pacific, indicating birds serving as a navigational aid in prehistoric antiquity as they were still being used by early medieval Norse seafarers. The most specific reference occurs in *Floki's Saga,* set down in the thirteenth century but recording events of four hundred years earlier, and describes three ravens consecrated to the gods carried aboard Floki's longship as land-finders. There is saga evidence to show other northmen doing likewise and it has been suggested that ravens, birds held by the Norse to be sacred to the god Odin, may have been specially trained for such a navigational role.

There is no evidence for ornithology as a science or pastime of the early middle ages, but orthomancy or belief in the magical significance of birds was widely practised in the druidic culture of Celtic Ireland. The association of a saint with his own species of bird — that of Columba with the "crane" (in fact, the grey heron) confirmed by Adamnan and elaborated by the later Irish sources being the best example — indicates

pre-Christian bird magic to have been passed into early
Christian Irish tradition. Similarly, Brendan has a
traditional association with the crow, but the significance of his consultation on the "Paradise of Birds" can
be taken as more practical than mystical, and especially when the course of his voyage follows so closely
a major spring migration route passing along the west
coast of Scotland and on to Iceland by way of the
Faeroes.

Close encounters between saints and birds appear to
have been less frequent in the Hebrides and north
Atlantic, at least on the evidence of the early sources,
than those of holy men with the great whales. Angus
Gunn's legend of Ronan and the *cionaran-crò* stands in
a long line of direct descent from Adamnan, who tells
of Columba's foreknowledge of a "whale of huge and
amazing size" at large in the deep waters between Iona
and Tiree and advising two priests of the potential
hazard to their safe crossing. Disregarding the saint's
advice, one of the two only just escapes his curach
being swamped by the wash of the breaching whale,
but the other — none other than Baithene, Columba's
fosterling — proclaims his faith that "the beast and I
are in the power of God" and stands forward in his
curach when the whale rises out of the depths to bless
the creature before it plunges beneath the waves.

The cetacean encounters in the Brendan sources are
all of them more dramatic than any found in Adamnan,
but the most bizarre occurs in the *Navigatio* when the
saint's curach approaches a whale so huge that his
companions think it an island. They bring their craft
alongside and come "ashore" to spend the night before
Easter Day on apparently dry land. After the morning
offices, Brendan's companions begin to prepare a meal,
but the saint himself has already returned aboard the

curach "for he knew well what manner of island this was." When they light a cooking fire on its back, the whale begins to move off and the terrified monks scramble into their curach just in time to watch their "island" swimming off into the distance.

There were, of course, very many more whales in those northern waters in the time before the industrial plundering of the ocean by more recent generations of humankind brought them almost to the point of extinction, but there is another factor, suggested to me by an interested naturalist, which might have its own peculiar bearing on encounters between cetaceans and seafaring saints. Whales and dolphins project and retrieve complex patterns of sound across great distances through the ocean, thereby seeking out both sustenance and society by means of echo-location. Their "sonar," then, would detect the alien character of a vessel formed of timber or metal, while a hide-hulled curach would return a quite different sensation and one perhaps resonant of the familar presence of their own living kind.

It might still be possible to discern a spiritual dimension in the relationship between the holy man and the species Brendan himself described as "the greatest of all creatures that swim in the sea." It is one which might be evoked by an awed tribute set down by Herman Melville in his novel *Moby Dick:* "You feel the Deity and the dread powers more forcibly than in beholding any other living object in living nature."

Continuing along his "Brendan Track" from the Faeroes to Iceland, Severin observes once again the impressive correspondence between the landscape ahead and the evidence of his primary source: "The *Navigatio* states that St Brendan approached the fiery Island of the

Smiths from the south and there is ample evidence of
volcanic activity off Iceland's southern shore."[28] To
which might be added a note of the sinister, even
demonic, aspect — rooted, perhaps, in folk-memories
associating magical powers with the impact of the
earliest metalworking cultures on prehistoric Ireland —
which attended the metalsmith throughout ancient
Irish tradition and is reflected also in a prayer traditionally attributed to St Patrick invoking divine protection against "the spells of women, smiths and druids."
The same ancient terror recurs again when the *Navigatio* brings Brendan's curach within sight of southern
Iceland.

> They came within view of an island which was
> very rugged and rocky, covered over with slag,
> without trees or herbage, but full of smiths'
> forges. St Brendan said to the brethren: "I am
> much distressed about this island; I have no
> wish to enter it or even approach it — yet the
> wind is driving us directly towards it, as if it
> were the aim of our course." When they had
> passed on further, about a stone's cast, they
> heard the noise of bellows blowing like thunder
> and the beating of hammers on anvils and iron.
> Soon after one of the inhabitants came forth...all
> hairy and hideous and begrimed with fire and
> smoke. St Brendan armed himself with the sign
> of the Cross and said to the brethren: "Put on
> more sail and ply your oars that we may get
> away from this island." Hearing this the savage
> man rushed down to the shore bearing in his
> hand tongs with a burning mass of slag, of great
> size and intense heat, which he flung after the
> servants of Christ. It passed them at a furlong's

distance and, where it fell into the sea, it fumed
up like a heap of burning coals and a great
smoke arose as if from a fiery furnace. When
they had passed on about a mile beyond the spot
where this burning mass had fallen...the whole
island seemed one globe of fire and the sea on
every side boiled up and foamed like a cauldron
on a fire.

Beyond Iceland, the westward progress of Severin's
curach might be considered to have passed beyond any
reasonable orbit of the holy man in the Hebrides,
unless he can be considered to have followed Brendan
into the same "northern regions" where Cormac's third
voyage "extended beyond the limits of human wanderings." In fact, the correspondence of the later course of
his "Brendan Track" with the evidence of the *Navigatio*
and other sources carries with it implications of crucial
significance for the sea-road of the saints.

The "column in the sea...of the clearest crystal, the
colour of silver, as hard as marble" can only have been
a spectacular iceberg such as those Severin encountered at the edge of the Greenland ice-pack and drifting
south in the Labrador current. So too, the "darkness so
dense they could barely see one another" corresponds
to the fog-banks through which his curach *Brendan*
passed shortly before reaching Newfoundland in the
June of 1977. He had arrived there by way of the same
sea-road and aboard just such a leather boat as the
*Navigatio* describes Brendan having found his way to
the Land of Promise of the Saints fourteen centuries
before. If that Land of Promise of the early Irish
sources and the Vinland of the Norse sagas were, in
fact, continental north America, then Severin's "Brendan Voyage" demonstrated beyond any reasonable

doubt that St Brendan the Voyager could have crossed
the Atlantic to reach the same "New World" which was
not to be officially "discovered" until more than a
thousand years after his death.

Severin did take two seasons to accomplish his
voyage and felt his craft to have been undermanned by
its crew of five, but all the early sources insist on
Brendan's own voyaging having taken "seven years"
and the *Navigatio* numbers his crew as fourteen
monks, men fully prepared by the ascetic monastic life
for the inevitable privations of curach-borne Atlantic
seafaring. Severin himself observed that "the medieval
equipment on *Brendan* was often a match for its
modern equivalent, and occasionally superior to it
when used in the grindingly harsh conditions of an
open boat in the North Atlantic."[29]

There can be no reasonable doubt, then, that Brendan and his kind could have accomplished such a
voyage across the Atlantic, but to demonstrate that
he *could* have done so is not to prove that he actually
did.

The reputation of the historical Brendan of Clonfert
as an extraordinary seafarer is also beyond question
and there is an abundance of evidence to confirm his
extensive voyaging along the western seaboard of
Ireland and Scotland. References to his association
with Orkney and the Western Isles preserved in the
Scottish calendars point to his voyaging further into
the north Atlantic, perhaps even to the Faeroes where
pollen analysis has suggested an Irish presence before
AD 600 and local tradition claims Brandarsvik to have
been "St Brendan's Bay." The possibility of his having
reached Iceland cannot be categorically denied, but
speculation as to whether the historical Brendan might

have sought land still further to the west must lie outwith the scope of these pages.

There is a point of significance, and one often overlooked, in the fact that none of the Brendan sources claim for him the first discovery of any of the lands visited on his voyaging. The *Navigatio* and the oldest text of his Latin *Life* both tell of his first hearing of the Land of Promise from a monk who had already been there and whose own abbot had been there before him. When Brendan himself finally arrives at the promised land in the west he finds someone waiting there to greet and to guide him, a holy man, incidentally, who is invoked by the Irish *Litany of Pilgrim Saints:*

> The anchorite whom Brendan found before him
>     in the Land of Promise,
> with all the saints who fell in all the islands of
>     the ocean; *Per Iesum.*

Every single island on which Brendan's curach makes landfall — and the *Navigatio* mentions many more than have been included in the summary outline here — he finds occupied by one or more hermits of the ocean. More curious still is the implication of the very early stage in the history of the Irish church at which holy men had begun to seek such "deserts in the pathless sea." The most historical of all such references is that to the "Island of St Ailbe" where Brendan and his monks spend each Christmas with a community dwelling under a vow of silence on an island at the edge of the northern sea. Their superior, who alone of the twenty-four brethren is allowed to speak to the visitors, tells Brendan of their having been there "from the days of St Patrick and St Ailbe, our patriarchs, for eighty years until now."

> Neither old age nor bodily infirmity increase
> upon us here, neither do we need cooked food,
> nor are we oppressed with heat or distressed
> with cold; but we live here, as it were, in the
> paradise of God.

The presentation of a remote retreat in the north Atlantic as a fusion of the Christian paradise with the more ancient Celtic otherworld of Tír na n-Og is all the more extraordinary for its firm association with the historical Ailbe of Emly, whose obituary is entered in the *Annals of Innisfallen* at 528. One of the elder saints of Ireland and patron of Munster, it was he who is said to have petitioned the king of Cashel to grant the Aran islands to Enda. The *Life of Ailbe* is very late, a work dated to the twelfth century, but its statement of the saint's having retired to Thule in his old age preserves a voyage tradition of much greater antiquity which is also attested by two invocations from the *Litany of Pilgrim Saints:*

> Four and twenty men of Munster who went with
> Ailbe on the ocean to revisit the Land of Prom-
> ise, who are there alive till doom; *Per Iesum.*

> Twelve men who went with Ailbe to death; *Per
> Iesum.*

Many more "Pilgrim Saints" are invoked in the *Litany,* which has been shown to have been set down at the Irish monastery of Lismore in Waterford in the later eighth century. Some of its entries invoke saints whose great celebrity has survived all the centuries:

Twelve warriors who went with Columcille on
pilgrimage to Alba; *Per Iesum.*

Three score men who went with Brendan to seek
the Land of Promise; *Per Iesum.*

Other entries invoke names and voyage traditions
apparently well-known in the eighth century, but many
of them long since obscured and others now entirely
forgotten:

Twelve men with Morioc across the sea; *Per
Iesum.*

The twelve pilgrims who went with Maedoc of
Ferns across the sea; *Per Iesum.*

Alfinus the holy pilgrim, and Mochonoc and
Mochasco; *Per Iesum.*

The *Litany* is an extraordinary document, enigmatic
and informative in equal measure, but it does illustrate
three historical aspects of its theme. First of all, there
were many holy men of the ancient Irish church —
some even now held in high honour, others abandoned
to obscurity by the intervening centuries — whose
eminence hinged on their pursuit of the white martyrdom. It would seem that the same tradition, whether
expressed in terms of exile, voyage or "pilgrimage for
Christ," is as old as the earliest evidence for Christianity in Ireland. The third and, perhaps, most significant
aspect of the *Litany of Pilgrim Saints* is its emphasis
on the mystical nature of their pilgrimages, an aspect
which would itself have greatly contributed to their
historical obscurity. As with the druid before them,

knowledge of the more mystic experiences of the saints of Ireland seems always to have been restricted to a close circle of initiates. It was a custom of which the visions of Columba are, perhaps, the best-documented example, but the *Navigatio* surrounds Brendan's preparations for his voyage with a similar atmosphere of spiritual secrecy when it tells of his choosing fourteen companion voyagers, "taking them apart" from the rest of the community and "retiring with them into an oratory" to explain his great purpose.

# The sea-road to "farthest Thule"

All of which indicates something of the context within which the true historical significance of the Voyage of Brendan might be brought into focus. It can no longer be considered a fantastical fiction constructed by later medieval authors around the legendary voyage of one holy man, but must be recognized as a documentary record of the collective seafaring experience of the ancient Irish church over at least three hundred years on the sea-road of the saints.

G.J. Marcus, the modern historian of the earliest conquest of the northern ocean, has proposed their "venturing, stage by stage, out into the Atlantic."[30] The holy men of early Christian Ireland first sought out for their holy places the islands of their own western seaboard and soon afterwards followed the secular settlement of "the Irish in Britain" into Argyll and the southern Hebrides. The foundation on Iona established a religious and political power centre on the northern frontier of Scotic Dalriada and with it a forward base for those venturing ever further in search of a "desert in the pathless sea." Their quest for an ever more remote hermitage in the ocean was to lead them through the Western Isles, by way of Orkney and Shetland, to the land of Thule and the very edge of the frozen sea.

By reason of the nature of the evidence of the earliest sources, the precise chronology of the sea-road of the saints must remain for the most part uncertain, but there is reliable evidence that Irish monks were established on the Faeroes by the second quarter of the eighth century and certainly voyaging to Iceland no more than sixty years after that. The principal, if not sole, source of that reliable evidence is the Irish monk-geographer Dicuil who wrote his *Liber de mensura orbis terrae* ("Book of the measurement of the world") in the year AD 825.

He had been educated in the monastery on Iona — very probably as the pupil of Suibhne, who was its abbot from 766 to 772 — and there gained access to the first-hand evidence, which he was to later set down for posterity, of the northern extension of the sea-road of the saints.

> Off the coast of the island of Britain are many islands...but they are most numerous in the north and north-west. On some of these islands I have lived, on others set foot, of some had a sight, of others read...

Amongst them is the island known to Dicuil, from the classical geographers in whose works he shows himself to be widely read, as "farthest Thule."

> It is now thirty years since priests who lived in that island from the first day of February to the first day of August told me that not only at the

summer solstice, but in the days on its either
side, the setting sun hides itself at the evening
hour as if behind a little hill, so that no darkness occurs during that very short period of
time, but whatever task a man might wish to
perform, even picking the lice from out of his
shirt, he can manage it as well as in broad day-
light. And had they been on a high mountain,
the sun would have been at no time hidden from
them.

They are in error who have written that the
sea around this island is frozen, and that there
is continuous day without night from the vernal
to the autumn equinox, and vice versa, perpetual
night from the autumnal equinox to the vernal;
for those sailing at an expected time of cold have
made their way there, and dwelling on the island enjoyed always alternate night and day
other than at the time of the solstice. But beyond one day's sailing from there to the north
they found the frozen sea.

The full and precise, even colourful, detail of Dicuil's
testimony securely identifies his "farthest Thule" as
Iceland. He confirms Irish monks to have sailed there
around the year 795 and to have stayed on the island
from February 1st — the first day of the old Celtic
spring in an age when the climate is believed to have
been measurably kinder than it is now — to the
beginning of August, by which time the nights would
have been just long enough to navigate by the stars.
Dicuil does not indicate the voyage he describes as
especially unusual and not for a moment does he
suggest that it was the first. The implication must be
that there had been earlier voyages to a summer

hermitage on Iceland, and it would be reasonable to suggest their following on from earlier monastic settlements on the Faeroes, regarding which Dicuil has still more to say.

> There are many other islands in the ocean to the north of Britain which can be reached from the northernmost British isles [Orkney and, probably, Shetland] in two days' and nights' sailing with full sails and a constant fair wind.... On these islands [the Faeroes] hermits who have sailed from our Scotia [Ireland] have lived for nearly a hundred years.
>
> But even as they had been always uninhabited since the beginning of the world, so now they have been deserted by anchorites because of Norse pirates...

There is a sad irony in the fact of Dicuil writing those words in the sanctuary of the Frankish court, where he was one of the many Irish monks who had fled to the continent to escape the onslaught of those same Norse pirates.

The first true geographer of the sea-road of the saints had himself been driven from the western sea in the terrible time of the descent of the red martyrdom...

# AFTERWORD
# The Descent of the Red Martyrdom

*This is the red martyrdom to man,*
*endurance of a cross or destruction*
*for Christ's sake.*

THE CAMBRAI HOMILY

If the original text of the *Cambrai Homily* was composed on Iona, then its ideal of the white martyrdom of exile was surely inspired by Columba. If there is uncertainty surrounding its place of origin, there is none about its antiquity because the surviving manuscript of the *Homily* is known to have been set down in the later eighth century and the original as much as a hundred years earlier. There was, then, just one holy man of the Hebrides who could have served as the inspiration for its tenet of the red martyrdom, and he is also invoked, with his community, in the *Litany of Pilgrim Saints*.

Fifty-four men who went to martyrdom with Donnan of Eigg; *Per Iesum.*

The entry of the feast of "Donnan of cold Eigg" under  April 17th in the *Martyrology of Oengus* is accompanied by a note of the dark prophecy attributed to
Columba.

> This Donnan went to Columcille to make him
> his *anmchara,* or soul-friend, upon which Colum-
> cille said to him: "I shall not be soul-friend to a
> company of the red martyrdom, for thou shalt
> come to red martyrdom and thy people with
> thee;" and so it was fulfilled.
>
> Donnan went then with his people to the Heb-
> rides; and they took up their abode there.

Despite the impressive title of "St Donnan the Great"
accorded him in some early sources, very little is
known of his life or lineage. He must have been a
junior contemporary of Columba and may have been a
monk of Iona, but there is also evidence to associate
him with Whithorn on the Solway, a possibility which
would correspond to the Kildonan dedication in Galloway. The great majority of *Cill Donnáin* dedications are
found in the west — notably on Kintyre, Arran, Skye,
Uist, and, of course, Eigg — and in the Highlands
beyond the Great Glen.

"His chapels in eastern Sutherland and north-
eastern Aberdeenshire," suggests E.G. Bowen, "might
equally well have been reached by a sea voyage around
northern Scotland and by way of the Moray Firth —
following a route well-known from megalithic times....
It is clear that the group of ancient chapels bearing his
name in the Western Isles appears to have been
established from his base at Eigg, making the fullest
use of the sea-lanes."[31]

The island of Eigg, just five miles in length and lying

to the south-east of Rhum, was well sited on those seaways, offering a convenient harbour for a curach on voyage from the southern Hebrides to Skye. The distinctive profile of Donnan's island — known to Adamnan as *Egea insula* — is dominated by the prominence of its Scuir, a hill towering almost 1,290 feet above its southern end and indicated by its massive cap of lava as the legacy of an ancient volcanic eruption. The Scuir is possessed of its own distinctly menacing aspect and it is not difficult to imagine it looming ominously over the red martyrdom entered in the *Annals of Tigernach* at the year 618.

The burning of Donnan of Eigg on the fifteenth before the kalends of May (17th April), with a hundred and fifty martyrs.

Tigernach's "hundred and fifty" monks would suggest Donnan's *familia* as being much larger than was customary for what would appear to have been a community of hermits, and was probably an exaggeration in the light of other estimates recorded by the martyrologists. The eighth-century *Martyrology of Tallaght* commemorates "fifty-two" martyred with Donnan, the same figure entered in the *Martyrology of Donegal* and the *Martyrology of Gorman,* so it would be reasonable to estimate the true number of martyrs at around a third of Tigernach's estimate.

The legend blaming the destruction of Donnan and his community on a Pictish queen angered by their settling on the land used to graze her flocks cannot be considered historical, but it is very old and might well hint at territorial dispute as the motive for the massacre. Eigg lay within the domain of the ancient "broch culture" and if, as seems most likely, Donnan suffered

the red martyrdom at the hands of Pictish pirates, then
he might, perhaps, be said to have been the last victim
of the Fomoire, the sea-demons of the Irish myths and
sagas, who terrorized the western seaboard throughout
prehistoric antiquity.

The destruction of Donnan and his monks was an
isolated incident and neither did it extinguish the
monastic foundation on Eigg which continued long into
the eighth century, probably until the most terrible
descent of the red martyrdom on the Hebrides which is
first entered in the *Annals of Ulster* at AD 794:

> The devastation of all the islands of Britain by
> the heathens.

It is not known when the first longship out of Norway
might have come "west-over-sea," but the Scandinavian
sea-raiders known to history as "vikings" had certainly
established forward bases on Shetland and on Orkney
by the last decade of the eighth century. They had
struck at the great Northumbrian monastery on Lindisfarne in 793 and the annalist's entry at 794 confirms
their breaking out into the Hebrides in the following
raiding season.

Dr Alfred Smyth's important history of early Scotland points to "all the evidence suggesting that the
Scottish Isles bore the full brunt of the fury of these
invaders who were instantly conspicuous to Scots,
English and Irish alike for their brutality and heathen-
ism.... Clearly the days of monasteries such as Eigg,
Applecross and countless other communities throughout the north and west were now numbered. Iona was
constantly exposed to viking marauders. Its position on
the western seaways and near the mouth of the firth of
Lorn, which gave it such a commanding position in the

days of Columba, now spelt its doom at the hands of sea-borne raiders."[32]

That doom is spelled out in the annalists' grim catalogue of the descent of the red martyrdom on the western sea. The *Annals of Innisfallen* at 795 record "the devastation of I-Columcille." The *Annals of Ulster* enter "the devastation of Rathlin and Skye pillaged and devastated" in the same year and "great incursions by the heathens in Erin and in Alba" at 798. Worse, much worse, was yet to come in 802 at which date the Ulster annalist records "I-Columcille burned by the heathens."

Cellach, abbot of Iona, returned urgently to Ireland to prepare a sanctuary for his community. Land was granted him at Kells in Meath in 804 and the annalist confirms "the building of a new monastery of Columcille" at Kells to have been under way by 807, but not in time to save the many monks of Iona whose massacre is entered in the *Annals of Ulster* at 806.

The community of I-Columcille slain by the heathens, that is, to the number of sixty-eight.

Soon afterwards, probably in 807, Cellach, the nineteenth abbot of Iona, evacuated his community to the comparative safety of Kells. Some modest monastic presence was evidently still maintained on the island and Cellach himself retired from the abbacy of Kells towards the end of his life in order to return to Iona where he died in 814.

Ten years later, the holy island of I-Columcille, for so long the most sacred shrine of the western sea, had come to represent the "Golgotha of the Gael" when Blathmac, warrior-turned-monk, arrived on Iona with the intention of seeking the red martyrdom — according to a closely contemporary account — "under his vow

to suffer the scars of Christ." So it was to be, on the
evidence of the obituary entered in the *Annals of Ulster*
at 825:

> The martyrdom of Blathmac, Fland's son, by the
> heathens in I-Columcille.

The historical record of the Celtic holy man in the
Hebrides dwindles to virtually nothing after the evacuation of Iona, but it is not difficult to imagine what
fate would have been inflicted by a viking warband
upon a hermit community discovered in the sea-girt
isolation of, for example, the distant island of Rona.


It was the death-dealing dragonship of the northmen,
then, which swept the holy men from the western sea,
but history does have a way of revealing strange
ironies with its great benefit of hindsight and one such
irony might serve here by way of epilogue.

Within a generation of the first raid on Iona, the
"islands of Britain" were known to the annalist as
*Innsegall,* the "islands of the aliens." The land-seeker
who came in the wake of the viking had so soon settled
into the islands and among the islanders of the Hebrides that, by the mid-ninth century, there are references in the Irish annals to *gall-gaedhil* or "alien
Gaels," effectively "Hebridean Norse." It took only some
two generations for Christianity to gain ground among
such a people and the first Hebridean Norse convert to
be noticed by the early sources was a daughter of a
chieftain of the Innsegall, one Aud called *djúpaudga,*
the "deep-minded." She was, for a time, the wife of a
Norse king of Dublin, but after her separation from
him returned to the Hebrides with her son, Thorstein,

who went on to carve out a territory for himself in Caithness in alliance with the Orkney Norse.

"Aud was in Caithness," according to a later saga account, "when she heard tell of Thorstein's death (c.875). She had a ship built secretly in the forest, and once she was ready hoisted sail for Orkney.... After that she set off to seek Iceland" taking with her Thorstein's son, more of her kinsfolk, and freed slaves of Celtic stock. "She made her home at Hvamm and had a place for her devotions at Krossholar, for she had been baptized and held strongly to the Christian faith." Aud the Deep-minded is remembered in Icelandic tradition as the founding matriarch of one of its great dynasties and it is said by one of the later sagas that her last wish was to be laid to rest at the very edge of the sea where each tide would wash over her grave, because the Icelandic Norse were turning away from her faith and she was anxious that she should not be buried in unconsecrated ground.

The saga history of the Icelandic settlement has been greatly distorted by its medieval authors, but modern research has shown that the first wave of Norse settlers in the land known to Dicuil just half a century earlier as Thule had come there, directly or otherwise, from the Hebrides and by way of the sea-road of the saints. In that light and although beyond possibility of proof, it has been suggested that perhaps "Aud and her kind had learned as much of wind and wave as of *pater* and *credo* from the voyager-monks whose sea-road they followed to Iceland and, another hundred years later, to Greenland and beyond."[33]

# References

1. L. Bieler, *Ireland: Harbinger of the Middle Ages*, p.4.
2. *The Martyrology of Gorman*, ed. W. Stokes, under March 17.
3. J. Streit, *Sun and Cross*, p.158.
4. K.H. Jackson, *The Oldest Irish Tradition: A Window on the Iron Age*.
5. Adamnan, *Life of Columba*, trans. W. Reeves, 2nd Preface.
6. V.G. Childe, *Scotland before the Scots*, p.46.
7. G.J. Marcus, *The Conquest of the North Atlantic*, pp.9, 21.
8. A. Ritchie, *Scotland BC*, p.49.
9. A.A.M. Duncan, *Scotland: The Making of the Kingdom*, 1978, p.42.
10. J.R. Allen & J. Anderson, *The Early Christian Monuments of Scotland*, 1993, ii, p.391.
11. W.J. Watson, *The History of the Celtic Placenames of Scotland*, 1986, p.87.
12. J.F. Kenney, *Sources for the Early History of Ireland: Ecclesiastical*, 1968, p.394.
13. J. Anderson, *Scotland in Early Christian Times*, p.80.
14. W.J. Watson, *The History of the Celtic Placenames of Scotland*, 1986, p.82f.
15. A.P. Smyth, et al., *Biographical Dictionary of Dark Age Britain*, p.4.
16. W.F. Skene, *Celtic Scotland*, ii, p.131.
17. W.J. Watson, *The History of the Celtic Placenames of Scotland*, 1986, p.87.
18. T. Severin, *The Brendan Voyage*, 1979, p.258f.
19. M.J.H. Robson, *Rona: The Distant Island*, p.2.
20. J.F. Kenney, *op.cit.*, p.301.
21. D.H. Farmer, *The Oxford Dictionary of Saints*, p.141.
22. C.D. Morris, *Church and Monastery in the Far North*, p.11f.
23. J.F. Kenney, *op.cit.*, p.410.
24. D.C.P. Mould, *The Irish Saints*, p.39.
25. *The Martyrology of Donegal*, ed. Todd & Reeves, under May 16.
26. J.F. Kenney, *op.cit.*, p.409.
27. Details abstracted from the technical appendices in T. Severin, *The Brendan Voyage*, 1979, pp.280-92.
28. T. Severin, *op.cit.*, p.163.

29.  T. Severin, *op.cit.,* p.260.
30.  G.J. Marcus, *The Conquest of the North Atlantic,* p.28f.
31.  E.G. Bowen, *Saints, Seaways and Settlements,* p.75f.
32.  A.P. Smyth, *Warlords and Holy Men: Scotland AD 80-1000,*
     1989, p.146.
33.  J. Marsden, *The Fury of the Northmen,* p.130.

# A Hebridean Calendar of Saints

The anniversary of the death of a saint was, and still is, the day on which the church of which he was the founder or patron celebrated the festival of his "ascent to the Kingdom."

Since at least as early as the eighth century, the dates of these festivals were compiled — with accompanying entries of praise-poetry, hagiographical tradition, or genealogy — into *félire* or "martyrologies," the "calendars of saints" which remain one of the most valuable sources for the history of the ancient Irish church. While there are a number of Irish *félire* and Scottish martyrologies, I have yet to come upon any Hebridean calendar of saints.

What follows has been compiled from the most ancient sources to list the feast days (where known) commemorating all those holy men for whom the foregoing pages have claimed any historical association with the western sea.

*January*
3    Findlugan, of Finlaggan on Islay

*February*
24   Cummene Ailbe, seventh abbot of Iona

*March*
2    Fergna, fourth abbot of Iona
5    Ciaran of Saigir
17   Beccan of Rhum
18   Comman, of Kilchoman on Islay

*April*
18   Donnan of Eigg
21   Maelrubha of Applecross

*May*
10   Comgall of Bangor
16   Brendan of Clonfert, "the Voyager"
18   Bresal, seventeenth abbot of Iona

*June*
9    Columba of Iona
     Baithene, second abbot of Iona
21   Cormac "of the Sea"
25   Moluag of Lismore

*July*
24   Blathmac, martyr of Iona

*August*
12   Segine, fifth abbot of Iona

*September*
12   Ailbe of Emly
23   Adamnan, ninth abbot of Iona

*October*
11   Cainnech of Aghaboe
27   Odhran "of Iona"

# Chronology

*Abbreviations*
Where the date chosen is significantly controversial, its source is indicated by:

| | |
|---|---|
| AI | *Annals of Innisfallen* |
| ATig | *Annals of Tigernach* |
| AU | *Annals of Ulster* |
| HE | Bede's *Historia Ecclesiastica* |

| | |
|---|---|
| c.394 | Pelagius the heresiarch in Rome |
| c.398 | Foundation of Whithorn by Ninian |
| | |
| 410 | Withdrawal of Roman army from Britain |
| 431 | Mission of Palladius to "the Irish believing in Christ" |
| 493 | Death of Patrick *(ATig)* |
| 498 | Migration of royal house of Dalriada to Kintyre |
| | |
| 501 | Death of Fergus mac-Erc, king of Dalriada |
| 521 | Birth of Columba at Gartan in Donegal |
| pre-524 | Foundation of Ailech by Brendan on the Garvellachs |
| 524 | Death of Brigid of Kildare *(AU)* |
| 528 | Death of Ailbe of Emly *(AI)* |
| c.530-c.560 | Brendan's voyages into the north Atlantic |
| 546 | Foundation of Derry by Columba *(AU)* |
| c.555-584 | Bruide mac-Maelchon, king of Picts |
| 557 | Foundation of Bangor by Comgall |
| 559/60 | Pictish war on Scotic Dalriada |
| | Death of Gabran, king of Dalriada |
| c.560-c.580 | Cormac's voyages into the north Atlantic |
| c.561 | Foundation of Clonfert by Brendan *(AI)* |
| 561 | Battle of Culdrevny |
| c.562 | Foundation of Lismore by Moluag |

| | |
|---|---|
| 563 | Columba's arrival in Scotland |
| 563/4 | Foundation of Hinba by Columba |
| | Comgall on Tiree |
| 565 | Foundation of Iona by Columba *(HE)* |
| 574 | Death of Conall, king of Dalriada "who gave Iona to Columcille" |
| | Ordination on Iona of Aidan mac-Gabran as king of Dalriada |
| 575 | Convention of Drumceat |
| 577 | Death of Brendan of Clonfert *(AU)* |
| c.590 | Death of Cormac ua-Liathan |
| 592 | Death of Moluag of Lismore |
| 597 | Death of Columba of Iona |
| | |
| 600 | Death of Baithene, abbot of Iona |
| | Death of Cainnech of Aghaboe |
| 601 | Death of Comgall of Bangor |
| 603 | Aidan mac-Gabran's invasion of Northumbria defeated at Degsastan |
| 605-623 | Fergna, abbot of Iona |
| 608 | Death of Aidan mac-Gabran in monastic retirement at Kilkerran on Kintyre |
| 618 | Martyrdom of Donnan of Eigg |
| 623-652 | Segine, abbot of Iona |
| 635 | Foundation of Lindisfarne from Iona |
| 657-669 | Cummene Ailbe, abbot of Iona |
| 664 | Synod of Whitby |
| c.664-669 | Cummene's *Life of Columba* |
| 671 | Maelrubha's arrival in Scotland |
| 672-693 | Bruide mac-Beli, king of Picts |
| 673 | Foundation of Applecross by Maelrubha |
| 677 | Death of Beccan of Rhum |
| 679-704 | Adamnan, abbot of Iona |
| 685 | Battle of Nechtansmere |
| 686-688 | Adamnan's visits to Northumbria |
| 688-692 | Adamnan's *Life of Columba* |
| | |
| 704 | Death of Adamnan on Iona |
| 716 | Adoption of "Roman" Easter on Iona |

717        Expulsion of monks of Iona from Pictland

722        Death of Maelrubha of Applecross

732        Bede's *Historia Ecclesiastica*

735        Death of Bede

772-801   Bresal, abbot of Iona

794        First outbreak of Norse viking raids in the Hebrides

795        Norse viking raids on Iona, Skye and Rathlin

c.800      *Martyrology of Oengus the Culdee*
            *Irish Litany of Pilgrim Saints*

802        Iona burned by Norse vikings

806        Massacre of sixty-eight monks in Norse viking raid on Iona

807        Transfer of abbot and community of Iona to Kells

c.825      Dicuil's *Liber de mensura orbis terrae*

825        Martyrdom of Blathmac in viking raid on Iona

847-858   Kenneth mac-Alpin, king of Scots

875        Migration of Aud the Deep-Minded and Hebridean Norse to Iceland

# Bibliography

*Abbreviations*

PSAS  *Proceedings of the Society of Antiquaries of Scotland*
SAF *Scottish Archaeological Forum*


Adamnan *see* Anderson & Anderson; Marsden & Gregory; Reeves & Skene.

Allen, J.R. & Anderson, J. *The Early Christian Monuments of Scotland,* Edinburgh 1903; rep. Forfar 1993.

Anderson, A.O. (ed./trs.) *Early Sources of Scottish History AD 500-1286,* Edinburgh 1922; rep. Stamford 1990.

—, & Anderson, M.O. (ed./trs.) *Adomnan's Life of Columba,* London 1961.

Anderson, J. *Scotland in Early Christian Times,* Edinburgh 1881.

Barber, J. *Innsegall: The Western Isles,* Edinburgh 1985.

Bieler, L. *Ireland: Harbinger of the Middle Ages,* Oxford 1963.

Bowen, E.G. *Saints, Seaways and Settlements in Celtic Lands,* Cardiff 1977.

Carmichael, A. *Carmina Gadelica,* Edinburgh 1928; rep. (English only edition) Edinburgh 1993.

Chadwick, N.K. *The Age of Saints in the early Celtic Church,* London 1961.

Childe, V.G. *Scotland before the Scots,* London 1946.

Davidson, H.E. (ed.) *The Seer: Studies in the Celtic Tradition,* Edinburgh 1989.

Delaney, F. *The Celts,* London 1986.

Drummond, J. *Sculptured Monuments of Iona & the West Highlands,* Edinburgh 1881; rep. Felinfach 1994.

Duncan, A.A.M. *Scotland: The Making of the Kingdom,* Edinburgh 1975; rep. Edinburgh 1978.

Ellis, P.B. *Celtic Inheritance,* London 1985.

Farmer, D.H. *Oxford Dictionary of Saints,* Oxford 1987.

Fraser, I.A. *The Place-Names of Argyll: An Historical Perspective,* Inverness 1988.

Graham, R.C. *The Carved Stones of Islay,* Glasgow 1895.

Herbert, M. *Iona, Kells & Derry: History and Hagiography of the Monastic Familia of Columba,* Oxford 1988.

Hopkin, A. *The Living Legend of St Patrick,* London 1989.

Hornell, J. "The Role of Birds in Early Navigation," *Antiquity* 20, Gloucester 1946.

Hughes, K. *Early Christian Ireland: Introduction to the Sources,* London 1972.

—, "On an Irish Litany of Pilgrim Saints," *Analecta Bollandiana* 87, 1959.

Hutton, R. *The Pagan Religions of the Ancient British Isles,* Oxford 1991.

Jackson, K.H. *Language and History in Early Britain,* Edinburgh 1953.

—, *The Oldest Irish Tradition: A Window on the Iron Age,* Edinburgh 1964.

Johnson, S. & Boswell, J. *Journey to the Western Islands & A Tour to the Hebrides,* Oxford 1930.

Johnstone, P. "The Bantry Boat," *Antiquity* 38, Gloucester 1964.

Jones, G. *The Norse Atlantic Saga,* Oxford 1986.

Kenney, J.F. *Sources for the Early History of Ireland: Ecclesiastical,* Columbia 1929; rep. Dublin 1968.

Kermack, W.R. *Historical Geography of Scotland,* Edinburgh 1926.

Killanin, Lord & Duignan, M.V. *The Shell Guide to Ireland,* London 1989.

Laing, L. & Laing, J. *Guide to Dark Age Remains in Britain,* London 1979.

Lamont, W.D. *Ancient & Medieval Sculptured Stones of Islay,* Glasgow 1972.

Lethbridge, T.C. *Herdsmen and Hermits: Celtic Seafarers in Northern Seas,* Cambridge 1950.

MacCullough, J.A. *The Religion of the Ancient Celts,* Edinburgh 1911; rep. London 1990.

Macdonald, A. "Two Major Early Monasteries of Scottish Dalriata: Lismore and Eigg," *SAF* 5, 1978.

Maceachearna, D. *The Lands of the Lordship,* Port Charlotte, Islay 1976.

Mackinley, W. *Ancient Church Dedications in Scotland,* Edinburgh 1914.

McNeill, F.M. *Iona: A History of the Island,* Glasgow 1920; rep. Moffat 1991.

—, *An Iona Anthology,* Glasgow 1952; rep. Iona 1990.

Mac Niocaill, G. *Ireland before the Vikings,* Dublin 1972.

Macquarrie, A. *Iona through the Ages,* Coll 1983.

Marcus, G.J. *The Conquest of the North Atlantic,* Woodbridge, Suffolk 1980.

Marsden, J. *The Fury of the Northmen: saints, shrines and sea-raiders in the Viking age,* London 1993.

—, *The Tombs of the Kings: An Iona Book of the Dead,* Felinfach 1994.

—, & Gregory, J. (ed./trs.) *The Illustrated Bede,* London 1989.

—, *The Illustrated Columcille,* London 1991.

Martin, M. *A Description of the Western Islands of Scotland,* 1716; rep. Edinburgh 1981.

Morris, C.D. *Church and Monastery in the Far North: An Archaeological Evaluation,* Jarrow 1990.

Mould, D.C.P. *Scotland of the Saints,* London 1952.

—, *The Irish Saints,* London & Dublin 1964.

Mytum, H. *The Origins of Early Christian Ireland,* London 1992.

O'Donoghue, D. *Lives and Legends of St Brendan the Voyager,* Dublin 1893; rep. Felinfach 1994.

O'Kelleher, A. & Schoepperle, G. (ed./trs.) *Betha Colaim Chille: Life of Columcille,* compiled by Manus O'Donnell, Urbana, 1918.

Piggott, S. *Scotland before History,* Edinburgh 1982.

Plummer, C. (ed./trs.) *Vita Sanctorum Hiberniae,* Oxford 1922.

Pringle, D., et al. *The Ancient Monuments of the Western Isles,* Edinburgh 1994.

Rees, A. & B. *Celtic Heritage: Ancient Tradition in Ireland and Wales,* London 1961.

Reeves, W. "St Maelrubha: His History and Churches," *PSAS* iii, 1861.

—, & Skene, W.F. (ed./trs.) *Adamnan's Life of Columba, founder of Hy,* Edinburgh 1874.

Ritchie, A. *Scotland BC,* Edinburgh 1988.

—, & Breeze, D. *Invaders of Scotland,* Edinburgh 1991.

Ritchie, G. & Harman, M. *Exploring Scotland's Heritage: Argyll and the Western Isles,* Edinburgh 1985.

Robson, M.J.H. *Rona: The Distant Isle,* Stornoway 1991.

Severin, T. *The Brendan Voyage,* London 1978; rep. London 1979.

Seymour, S-J.D. *Irish Visions of the Otherworld,* London 1930.

Shea, M. *Britain's Offshore Islands,* Richmond, Surrey 1981.

Simpson, W.D. *The Historical Saint Columba,* London 1927.

—, *The Celtic Church in Scotland,* Aberdeen 1935.

Skene, W.F. *Celtic Scotland: A History of Ancient Alban,* Edinburgh 1886-90.

—, *see also* Reeves, W.

Smyth, A.P. *Warlords and Holy Men: Scotland AD 80-1000,* London 1984; rep. Edinburgh 1989.

—, *see also* Williams, A.

Stokes, W. (ed./trs.) *Lives of the Saints from the Book of Lismore,* Oxford 1890.

—, *The Annals of Tigernach,* Paris 1895-6; rep. Felin-fach 1993.

—, *The Martyrology of Gorman,* London 1895.

—, *The Martyrology of Oengus the Culdee,* London 1905.

Streit, J. *Sun and Cross,* Edinburgh 1984.

Swire, O.F. *The Outer Hebrides and their Legends,* Edinburgh & London 1966.

Thomson, W.P.L. *History of Orkney,* Edinburgh 1987.

Tierney, J.J. (ed./trs.) *Dicuil, Liber de mensura orbis terrae,* Dublin 1967.

Todd, J.H. & Reeves, W. (ed.) *The Martyrology of Donegal: A Calendar of the Saints of Ireland,* Dublin 1864.

Trenholme, E.C. *The Story of Iona,* Edinburgh 1909.

Watson, W.J. *The History of the Celtic Placenames of Scotland,* Edinburgh 1926; rep. Dublin 1986.

Williams, A., Smyth, A.P. & Kirby, D.P. *Biographical Dictionary of Dark Age Britain,* London 1991.

Wright, G. *Jura's Heritage: A Brief History of the Island,* Jura 1991.

# Index

Adamnan, abbot of Iona
49–51, 74, 81, 90f
Aidan mac-Gabran, king of
Dalriada 62, 69, 110–13,
136f
Ailbe of Emly, St 20, 38,
181f
Applecross see Maelrubha, St
Aran Islands see Enda, St
Arran 43, 118, 190
Aud the Deep-minded 194f

Baithene, abbot of Iona
94–96, 100, 109, 113,
133, 139, 176
Beccan of Rhum 152f
Bede, The Venerable 54,
56, 61f, 136, 147
Blathmac 193f
Brendan the Voyager, St 77,
114–21, 125, 127, 141,
150, 153f, 160, 164–82
Bresal, abbot of Iona 91
Brigid of Kildare, St 31,
119f, 167
Bruide mac-Beli, king of
Picts 81
Bruide mac-Maelchon, king
of Picts 57f, 61f, 124f,
141f

Cainnech of Aghaboe, St
72–78, 114–16, 119, 121f,
124f, 127

Callanish stones, Lewis 44
Campbeltown (Kilkerran),
Kintyre 64, 68f
Ciaran of Clonmacnois, St
59, 65, 96
Ciaran of Saigir, St 20, 38,
63–69, 78, 115
Coemgen of Glendalough,
St 53, 104
Colonsay 76, 77, 103
Columba (Columcille), St
44, 48–54, 58–63, 83, 95,
107–14, 124–27, 130–37,
141f, 154–56, 175f
Comgall of Bangor, St 79,
115f, 122–27
Comman 86–87
Cormac, St 114–17, 125–
27, 142, 153–61
Corryvreckan 76, 83
Cúchulainn 35, 43
Cummene, abbot of Iona 87f
curach 44f, 139f, 171–73

Dalriada 41–43, 54–58,
113, 134–37
Dicuil 185–87
Donnan of Eigg, St 189–92
druids 30f, 109f
Dunadd, Kintyre 54f

Eigg 139, see also Donnan,
St
Eithne, St 83–86, 105

Enda of Aran, St  31, 150,
    182
Ernan  101, 104–6

Fair Isle  161
Faeroe Islands  77, 174–75,
    180, 185, 187
Fergna (Virgnous), abbot of
    Iona 86f
Fergus mac-Erc, king of
    Dalriada  55–57, 60, 68,
    111, 134
Findlugan see Finlaggan
Finlaggan, Islay  97f
Finn mac-Cumaill  35, 43,
    166
Finnian of Clonard, St  31,
    59, 72f
Foula  161

Garvellachs  84, 102f, 118f,
    167

Harris  81, 164
'Hinba' see Jura

Iceland  77, 161, 176, 178,
    180, 185–87, 195
Inchkenneth  121f
Iona  44, 61, 63, 91, 129–43,
    151, 176, 184, 192–94
Ireland, coming of Chris-
    tianity to,  15–23
—, monastic church in,
    27–29
—, mythic history of,  32–39
—, tribal society of,  24–27
Islay  43, 48, 65, 69f, 71–98,
    118

Jura  48, 99–127, 133, 135,
    139, 167

Kilarrow, Islay  78–80
Kilchiaran, Islay  69, 78
Kilchoman, Islay  86
Kildalton, Islay  91–96, 132
Kilkerran see Campbeltown
Killernandale, Jura  104–7
Kilmeny, Islay  83f, 105
Kintyre  47–70, 73, 111,
    118, 139, 190

Lewis  44, 145–48, 149, 164
Lindisfarne, Northumber-
    land  89–91, 192
Lismore, Lorn see Moluag, St

Maelrubha of Applecross, St
    79–83
Manannan mac-Lir  39
martyrdom  14, see also red
    martyrdom and white
    martyrdom
Moluag of Lismore, St
    162–64
monasticism  27–29
Mull  100, 122, 136, 163

Ninian of Whithorn, St  22f,
    27

Odhran, St  131–32
Orkney  34, 112, 117, 125,
    127, 156f, 164, 180, 185,
    192, 195

Paschal Controversy, the
    88–91

Patrick, St 18–23, 38, 44, 65f, 71, 119, 129, 178, 181
Pelagius 22
Picts 41, 57f, 61f, 81, 123–25, 135
Pytheas 43, 99, 161f

Raasay 80, 163
Rathlin Island 43, 76, 193
red martyrdom, the 14, 189–93
Rhum *see* Beccan
Rona, North 146–49
Ronan, St 143, 145–49, 176

St Kilda 117, 173f
Segine, abbot of Iona 87, 89f, 152
Seil 118
Severin, Tim 77, 142, 171–74, 177–80
Shetland 34, 162, 185, 192
Skellig Michael, Kerry 150

Skye 43, 80, 100, 163, 190, 193
Sula Sgeir 150
Tarbert, Jura 103, 106–7, 126
Texa, off Islay 75f, 78, 126
Thule 161f, 164, 182, 184–87
Tiree 63, 95, 121–23, 126, 133f, 137, 139, 176

Uists, the 174, 190

viking raids 192–94

Western Isles, the 34, 43, 127, 145–51, 161, 163–64, 173, 180, 185, 190
whales & 'sea monsters' 119f, 158–61, 176f
white martyrdom, the 13–15, 37f
Whithorn 190, *see also* Ninian, St

# Power of Raven, Wisdom of Serpent

## Celtic Women's Spirituality

### Noragh Jones

*Power of Raven be thine,*
*Wisdom of Serpent be thine,*
*Wisdom of valiant Eagle*
　　From *A Good Wish* in the *Carmina Gadelica*

The customs and spirituality of the traditional communities of the Highlands and Islands of Scotland were handed down for centuries through their oral culture. Much of their culture and folklore was recorded in the *Carmina Gadelica*. Their way of life preserved many aspects of spirituality and reverence for nature which have been lost to those who live in a modern urban environment.

Noragh Jones describes the vital roles of women in those communities and their customary powers of 'seeing,' healing, blessing, and cursing. She concludes that their deep wisdom and qualities of hospitality and conviviality, together with their celebration of the ordinary tasks of daily life, have much to teach us in our present-day urban communities.

Noragh Jones teaches courses in women's spirituality at the University of Aberystwyth.

Floris Books/Lindisfarne Press

# Carmina Gadelica

*Hymns and Incantations from the Gaelic*

*Collected and translated by* Alexander Carmichael
*and presented by* John MacInnes

*These religious texts with their strange blend of pagan
and Christian imagery, witnesses to the spirituality of
a vanished age, their complement of mysterious words
and phrases, apparently unknown outside this reposit-
ory of incantations, and their dignified, almost liturgical, style, fascinate the reading public.*

John MacInnes

The *Carmina Gadelica* is the most comprehensive collection of poems and prayers from the Gaelic tradition
of oral poetry. These poems had been handed down
through the generations in a living oral tradition. This
tradition and the way of life which sustained it have
now disappeared but these poems and prayers live on
to remind us of the faith of the unknown poets who
composed them.

Previously only available as a bilingual text in six
volumes, this one-volume edition in English only is an
important contribution to the wider awareness of Celtic
literature.

Floris Books/Lindisfarne Press

# The Illustrated Life of Columba

### John Marsden
Translation by John Gregory
Photography by Geoff Green

The great sixth-century saint and founder-abbot of Iona, St Columba — known throughout the Gaelic world as Columcille — left a mark on history that endures to this day far beyond the Celtic lands. A detailed account of his life and deeds has come down to us in the work of Adamnan, ninth abbot of Iona, who drew on the living memory of the saint's contemporaries.

John Marsden here provides a vivid description of the period, as well as a revealing portrait of the saint and his biographer. John Gregory's translation of Adamnan's *Life* is accompanied by Geoff Green's photographic portrait of the landscape and seascape in which Columba lived and in which his spirit still thrives.

### Floris Books